MW01288756

FOUR MONTHS
OF SUNDAYS

by Jim Nichols

ISBN: 9781719296472

PREFACE

This is a plain, nuts and bolts arrangement of 120 communion meditations -- brief, singular devotional thoughts based on Scriptures with applications intended for the Lord's Supper. You won't find a table of contents, since the first 110 meditations are simply numbered. The last ten appear at the end of the book under the classification, "Special Sundays."

Maybe you need something other than communion meditations. With a simple modification, you should be able to use these same thoughts for devotional thoughts when you are called upon to share one. Preachers could use each thought to expand into a sermon or to find usable illustrations.

They are brief, since that's what a devotional thought should be, not a three-point homily but a thought that can sink home in just a few words.

I pray these thoughts first become your own, as you read them. Then, I pray you will share them with others effectively. May we all grow together in the grace and knowledge of our Lord Jesus Christ!

Your servant and His,

Jim Nichols, 2018

1. AT THE CAPTAIN'S TABLE

"We have an altar from which those who minister at the tabernacle have no right to eat" (Hebrews 13:10).

If ever you have been on a cruise, you understand what a privilege it is to be invited to dine at the Captain's table.

If you've never been on a cruise, take my word for it. Even though I am married to the classy woman I am married to, we were never invited to dine at the Captain's table on our cruises!

The last chapter in the book of Hebrews closes out with this reminder to people who were being persecuted for leaving Judaism to become followers of Christ. Maybe being Jewish was a privilege, but being a Christian was a much greater privilege. Only the Jewish priests were allowed to eat meat offered on the altar of burnt offering. Only the priests could eat from the table of the shew bread.

But you and I eat around the table of the Lord. He is the Ultimate Sacrifice of sin for all men for all time! He is the Eternal High Priest serving not in the scale model of God's throne here on earth, but before the very Throne of God. Every week, we dine at the Captain's Table. Here, again, we dine in His presence as privileged people, made holy by the Blood of Jesus.

2. THE FRIEND OF SINNERS

"But the Pharisees and the teachers of the law muttered, 'This man welcomes sinners and eats with them'." (Luke 15:2).

Jesus' critics were hardest on Him because of the company He kept. To eat with someone was to show full acceptance of him. Even you and I could understand their concern that a respected Rabbi would allow himself to be associated with sinners.

But the charge sounded very good to the people gathered around Jesus! No one else in their society accepted them because of their sinful past. Jesus offered them acceptance despite it. They were recipients of a second chance.

To meet at the table of the Lord is to assemble as a motley group of outcasts and sinners accepted by the Lord and given another chance. We come unworthy. He makes us worthy. We share in this feast, acknowledging that his suffering and death were on our behalf. If we are sinners, He wants to be known as our Friend.

3. KING'S TABLE, KING'S FAMILY

"David asked, 'Is there anyone still left of the house of Saul to whom I can show kindness for Jonathan's sake?'" (II Samuel 9:1)

When one dynasty takes the place of another, the new regent usually secures the throne by getting rid of all other claimants to the throne. If you were part of the former dynasty, you either fled the country, or you were hunted down and exterminated.

Jonathan had one surviving son. With Saul and Jonathan dead and Ishbosheth foully murdered, David had ascended the throne over Israel. The one surviving son of Jonathan was named Mephibosheth, and if you wondered whether or not he had fled the country you need to understand that Mephibosheth was lame in his legs ever since he had suffered some kind of neurological injury at the age of five.

Put yourself in Mephibosheth's place: If you were the most direct claimant to the throne under the old dynasty and you were summoned before the new king, wouldn't you be afraid of what was about to happen to you?

Instead of death or banishment, Mephibosheth was shown favor for the sake of his Father, Jonathan. Though he was a lame beggar for all practical purposes, he would now be seated at the King's table to eat. His father's real estate holdings would be managed by Saul's former servants. He would be counted a member of the King's household from then on.

I cannot help but see the parallel between this beggar in II Samuel and our own plight. If the God of all Creation summoned us before Him, shouldn't we tremble? We deserve His wrath because of the rebellion in His creation! We are powerless to oppose Him and can only come in fear when He summons us.

But the God of all Creation instead shows us kindness for Jesus' sake. We are counted a part of His household, while angels are our ministering spirits. As a reminder of His constant kindness, we find ourselves seated here, at the King's table each First Day of the Week.

Who would've thought a lame beggar could ever be so honored?

4. AN INDESTRUCTIBLE LIFE

"And what we have said is even more clear if another priest like Melchizedek appears, one who has become a priest not on the basis of a regulation as to his ancestry but on the basis of the power of an indestructible life" (Hebrews 7:15, 16).

In Eugene O'Neill's play *Lazarus Laughed* the dreaded tyrant Caligula summons a man he learns claims to have been raised from the dead by Jesus and is telling people that Jesus Himself has been raised to die no more. Caligula has controlled the people by their fear of death at his hand.

O'Neill describes the confrontation this way: "Lazarus looks upon Caligula as a man in love with the Lord and says, 'Death is dead, Caligula! Death is dead!'"

The Lord's Supper commemorates the pivotal point in history where mankind was at its worst and God was at His finest. Where Satan and his host raged with suffering and death on a cross, God answered back with redemption, forgiveness, and the promise of an indestructible life.

What tyrant can threaten us now? Death is dead!

5. DISCERNING THE BODY

"For those who eat and drink without discerning the body of Christ eat and drink judgment on themselves" (I Corinthians 11:29).

The term "discerning" isn't used too often in our everyday conversation. How many will find it on Twitter or Facebook? It comes from insightful recognition. Paul told the Corinthian Christians that when we partake of the Lord's Supper, we need this insight, this recognition of the Body of Christ.

Then in the very next chapter he tells them, "Now you are the body of Christ, and each one of you is a part of it" (I Cor. 12: 27). He wasn't just speaking about remembering the physical body of Jesus with which He suffered on our behalf, he was talking about understanding that those around us partaking of the loaf are joined together with us as members of Christ's body, the church.

To discern the Body of Christ, we need to regard one another, to pray for one another, to cry when another cries, and rejoice when another rejoices. Communion is a sharing with one another, not a private meditation done in a vacuum.

As we partake, may we do so in a manner that recognizes the Body of Christ in our prayerful support of one another.

6. COME TO YOUR QUIET PLACE

"Then, because so many people were coming and going that they did not even have a chance to eat, he said to them, 'Come with me by yourselves to a quiet place and get some rest'" (Mark 6:31).

Amazing, though it seems, the era in which we live, the era of advanced technology and instant communication, is the era where we are busier than ever. Fewer people sleep adequately each night. More vacation time than ever before goes unused. Families have less and less supper time together.

It's not really a new phenomenon though. Even Jesus and His close Disciples had pressure like this. John had been executed in prison. Jerusalem's religious leaders had clamped down on Jesus' presence in Judea. Larger multitudes than ever clamored around Jesus in Galilee, but His hometown of Nazareth had tried to throw Him over the cliff!

In the middle of all this hubbub, Jesus told His disciples to draw away into a quiet place to get some rest. It's good advice for our pressured age too!

The Table of our Lord is a place where we shut out much of the world around us and draw close to Jesus. It is a quiet place where we escape the mundane and focus again on what really matters. Headphones off! Cell phones silent! Forget the texts and Twitters for awhile. Come into the quiet place. We all need the rest!

7. BACK TO BASICS

"He has shown you, O mortal, what is good. And what does the Lord require of you? To act justly and to love mercy and to walk humbly with your God" (Micah 6:8).

My son used to take me on backpacking trips – until I got too arthritic to finish the last one! Among the lessons to be learned from them, though, was the lesson of minimizing all we carry. Food, bedroll, sleeping mat, change of clothes. Someone would pack the tent, but it was small and light for two or three of us! One person took the garden trowel. Tissue was usually a packet or two of Kleenex pocket size. Everybody had his own tin cup for cooking, eating and drinking. Water? We had a 2 quart plastic bag of it and a filtered pump for getting more from streams and springs along the way.

If you were to condense God's expectations down to the basics, you might use the two basic commandments Jesus recited: Love God. Love your neighbor. The Prophet Micah boiled it down to three things: Act justly. Love mercy. Walk humbly with God.

When he says we are to act justly, he speaks about how we initiate our dealings with others. We treat the next person with respect and deal honestly.

When Micah tells us to love mercy, he speaks about how we respond when others don't deal justly with us. We all mess up. We all need forgiveness. If we don't show it, it won't be shown to us.

But most of all, we are reminded to walk with God in humility. It is here at the table of the Lord we see ourselves in the Eternal Perspective. God is totally just. Through Jesus, He extends us the grace and mercy we so need. We need His presence. In the body of Jesus which walked this earth we have His presence. In the blood of Jesus which was poured out on the cross, we have His justice and mercy in perfect balance.

8. WHERE IS THE ROOM?

"...Say to the owner of the house, 'The Teacher says, "Where is the guest room, where I may eat the Passover with my disciples?"'" (Luke 22:11).

The final Passover meal, Jesus' last supper with His close Disciples, was to happen this evening. He yearned for this supper with such a deep desire that the term for His suffering and death "The Passion" spring from this term.

To prepare for the meal, Jesus sent a couple disciples to find the place by a secret code. It apparently was prearranged by Jesus so He could not be arrested until the meal was over. The two disciples were to look for a man carrying a water jar – something women normally did. He would show them the room so they could get the elements of the meal ready that night.

Jesus has prearranged a place for us too! In the same evening, in that very room, He told the disciples, "I go to prepare a place for you. And if I am going to prepare a place for you I will certainly come again to take you to myself so that where I am you may also be!"

At the Lord's Table, we remember the institution of this Memorial Feast, but we look beyond it to see that there is another prearranged signal so that we may all have His answer to the question, "Where is the room that is prepared?"

9. "FEEL BAD" WORSHIP

"I tell you that this man, rather than the other, went home justified before God" (Luke 18:14a).

The Parable of the Pharisee and the Publican praying in the Temple should cause us to re-examine how we measure the success of worship. We live in a hedonistic society that even measures the worship of God by how good it makes us to feel. The Pharisee prayed a typical Pharisaical prayer that made him feel good about himself and his standing before God. The Publican was so ashamed he couldn't look up toward heaven and wept for mercy instead. His prayer time in the temple was tearful and miserable.

But the Publican went home justified, while the Pharisee didn't!

Mind you, they both went home feeling good, but only the Publican had a divine reason to feel that way. His many sins had been forgiven, and he was counted justified in God's eyes. The Pharisee had gone to the Temple already feeling justified in his own eyes. He went home feeling the same way he had come, and God hadn't changed anything about his miserable life for him!

Maybe some tears at the Lord's Table would be more beneficial for us than how good we feel from the music in the worship service. Maybe a call to repentance would help a true worshipper more than a sermon on getting into our "abundant life groove."

Jesus said, "Blessed are they who mourn, for they shall be comforted."

10. FOR CHRIST'S SAKE

"Be kind to one another, tenderhearted, forgiving one another, even as God for Christ's sake has forgiven you (Ephesians 4:32).

A man taking an automobile safari on a wildlife preserve in Kenya several years ago became annoyed at a car turned sideways in the road ahead of him, apparently looking at a herd of zebras. He honked his horn, but the car remained there. He rolled down his window and angrily shouted, "Where are you going, for Christ's sake?"

The window of the other car rolled down to reveal Billy Graham, who humbly smiled and said, "I go everywhere for Christ's sake!"

We gather around this table to remember how we achieved our right standing before God. It was not for our righteousness, not for our sakes that we are forgiven. It was for Christ's sake. While a cruel and impatient world around us may use the term "for Christ's sake" as one of many profanities, we are expected to reply with a blessing for the curse. And we do so for Christ's sake. For Christ's sake, we are forgiven. For Christ's sake we will forgive.

11. THE RING BEARER AND THE SIN BEARER

"God made him who had no sin to be sin for us, so that in him we might become the righteousness of God (II Corinthians 5:21).

A favorite fantasy based series that was made into a film series was J.R.R. Tokien's *The Lord of the Rings*. It's much too complex to cover even a good summary, but the major element is in the quest of a Hobbit named Frodo Baggins to carry the one ring of power and cast it into the fires of Mount Doom where it was forged so that the world of Middle Earth would be saved from evil. As the story unfolds, the burden of the ring is so great it becomes questionable whether or not Frodo will succeed in the task that has fallen to him.

Discerning eyes see in Frodo the Christ figure of the Suffering Servant, whose task is described at the end of II Corinthians 5 as being made sin on our behalf, even though He had no sin of His own. Frodo Baggins was the ring bearer in Tolkien's legend. But Jesus was the Sin Bearer in the eternal purposes of God.

The burden was heavy enough that Jesus confided, "My soul is exceedingly sorrowful, even unto death" shortly before He was arrested. How could you or I ever fathom what it was like to be counted guilty of the sins of everyone else when He had not even experienced personal sin?

There is much to ponder at the Table of the Lord, but the depth of God's grace and love and the burden of the sins of the world go beyond our comprehension.

12. FOREIGNERS AND EXILES

"Dear friends, I urge you as foreigners and exiles, to abstain from sinful desires, which wage war against your soul" (I Peter 2:11).

When our third child arrived from South Korea to live with us, we had to go through the usual procedures for her entering our country and home as a finally forever member of our family. Before her adoption was finalized, I was describing to a woman in our congregation how I had to carry her alien registration card until she could become a U.S. citizen. As I did this, her little five year-old's eyes got as large as saucers. He had only one image to associate with the word "alien," and it was something like an extra terrestrial!

I wonder if we get the right image about our pilgrimage here on earth. We really don't belong here. We have a different citizenship, and we need to be careful we remember our status. We are in enemy occupied territory right now, and we are susceptible to attacks on our well-being.

Peter reminds us that we are foreigners and exiles in our current world status. We need to draw sustenance from the homeland here at the Table of the Lord. Here we refocus. Here we are refreshed. Here we renew our allegiance to our true Homeland and its King.

May this loaf and cup at this table remind us who we are, why we are here, and where we are going!

13. WITHOUT GRUMBLING AND COMPLAINING

"Do everything without grumbling or arguing, so that you may become blameless and pure, "children of God without fault in a warped and crooked generation" (Philippians 2:14, 15).

Have you ever known someone who seemed addicted to his own adrenaline? You know the kind – always angry about everything, always bitter and complaining, forever whining about the way things are. It's not that there isn't room for improvement in our lives and in the world around us, but aren't we all better motivated by thanks and encouragement from one another for what we are doing right, rather than constant focus on what's wrong?

Jesus didn't say the world would believe in Him once they could see perfection in us. He certainly didn't say they would know us by our insistence on absolutely accurate doctrine or a high work ethic. He said they would believe in Him when they could see the identifying characteristic of our love for one another.

Perfection has been supplied for our deficiencies in the Perfect Lamb sacrificed for us. Judgment and correction will be afforded when He makes all things new at the end of time. In between those two major events in human history, the work of the Lord falls into the hands of His church. And our greatest task at hand is to love each other fervently, from the heart! We have a world that needs to know Jesus has sent us, and this Table is a point of renewal to our commitment to build one another up, all the more so as we see the Final Day approaching!

14. TRIUMPHING AT THE CROSS

"And having disarmed the powers and authorities, he made a public spectacle of them, triumphing over them by the cross" (Colossians 2:15).

There was a taunt sung by the British regulars during the Revolutionary War against the colonists. These poorly trained, poorly equipped men were the brunt of the song about "Yankee Doodle" who couldn't even keep step in marching and who only had farm horses and ponies for mounts in warfare. Imagine the words of "Yankee Doodle" sung with a British Cockney accent across the battle field to taunt the men on the other side. That's where the history of this tune began, but not where it ended.

When Cornwallis was defeated at Yorktown, and General Washington arranged the order of events for the surrender of Cornwallis' sword and his troops, Washington made it a point to have the fifes and drums strike up the song that had been their original taunt. These plow boys and farmers would see the British surrender to the tune of "Yankee Doodle." What had originally been thrown at them as a taunt, they threw back in a note of triumph.

In a larger sense, God has done this with the Cross. It marks history as the point where sinful man was at his worst. Yet we speak of a "Good Friday," because the Cross marks God's foolishness triumphing over the wisdom of man.

As we remember the suffering of our Lord in His body and His very death in His shed blood, may we glory in the Cross.

15. INCONCEIVABLE

"What no eye has seen, what no ear has heard, and what no human mind has conceived – the things God has prepared for those who love him."

Very few movies get quoted as much as *The Princess Bride*. One oft-repeated line (repeated often in the film itself) is Wallace Shawn's character, Vissinni's exclamation, "Inconceivable!" That line entered my mind when I read in this text that no human mind has conceived the things God has prepared for us.

Yes, heaven is that awesome, that *inconceivable*!

But when we gather around the Lord's Table, we need to acknowledge a few more "inconceivable" things first.

It is inconceivable that God loved us while we were still sinners in total rebellion against Him.

It is inconceivable that the Son would leave His Godness, His place in heaven, His fullness of deity to become one small part of His creation.

It is inconceivable that despite His own sinlessness He would be willing to submit to a kangaroo court and accept the sentence of undeserved death on a cross.

It is inconceivable that God had in His mind from the very beginning of creation the redemption of all mankind through this, mankind's worst day in God's face.

His Body suffering our deserved pain.

His Blood poured out in place of our lives.

The Creator dying for His creation – Inconceivable!

16. NO LONGER SERVANTS, BUT FRIENDS

"You are my friends if you do what I command. I no longer call you servants, because a servant does not know his master's business. Instead, I have called you friends, for everything that I learned from my Father I have made known to you" (John 15:14, 15)

Before the fall in Eden, God would walk with Adam in the cool of the day because this was God's connection with man. They were friends. But soon came the Fall, and the relationship was broken.

Did you ever have a close friend do you dirty and in so doing absolutely destroy the friendship? It's a peculiar grief that too many people experience, even Jesus. Judas was one of the Twelve, probably the most promising of all of them. So, if we really want to identify with our Lord, we should remember don't fully fellowship in His sufferings until we feel the sting of a betrayer's kiss on our cheek.

God first felt betrayal not in the Garden of Gethsemane, but in the Garden of Eden. Our friendship with Him was necessarily interrupted by our rebellion against Him. Even under the Law, that fellowship was strained at best, still fully broken at worst.

But now, as Jesus and the Eleven left the Upper Room and made their way out of the city walls up Olivet into the Garden of Gethsemane, He says they are no longer called His servants. A new relationship was about to be ushered in; or more correctly, the original relationship was about to be restored. Jesus had just made this often quoted line: "Greater love has no one than this: to lay down one's life for one's friends" (John 15:13).

God had grieved His broken friendship with man long enough. Now, in the grief He would feel in the cross of Jesus, that friendship would be restored. This memorial feast celebrates the restoration of a long-broken friendship.

17. THE GENTLE SAVIOR

"He will not shout or cry out, or raise his voice in the streets. A bruised reed he will not break, and a smoldering wick he will not snuff out" (Isaiah 42:2, 3).

Did you ever get those trick candles that won't blow out on your birthday cake? You blow the flames out, but they spring back to life!

Now, be honest: did you ever put those trick candles on someone else's birthday cake?

The candle wick is lightly impregnated with flecks of gun powder which ignite when the wick ember gets to them. The little spark emitted by a grain of gun powder ignites the vaporizing paraffin from the smoldering wick. To extinguish the Everlit candle you have to moisten your finger tips and pinch the wick, smothering the ember. As long as the ember glows in the wick, the possibility of rekindling the candle is there.

Jesus was described as a gentle servant who wouldn't break a bent reed or snuff out a smoldering wick. He is the One who rekindles the flame that is all but out. He binds up wounds. He forgives and restores. In Him we have hope when it might seem that all hope is gone.

In ten more chapters, Isaiah speaks of this same servant being like a sheep taken to the slaughter. He did not cry out. As God, He has the right to utter one word and smite all those opposed to Him, but as the Lamb of God He first has come to deal gently with fallen sinners. He is the Gentle Savior.

18. GLORYING IN THE CROSS

"May I never boast except in the cross of our Lord Jesus Christ, through which the world has been crucified to me, and I to the world" (Galatians 6:14).

In conventional wisdom, especially in the secular Roman world of Paul's day, there was nothing to boast about in a cross. It was a criminal's death with excruciating torture. Crucifixion was such an ugly death that no Roman citizen could be crucified, not matter how awful his crime. Nobody would willingly bring his own life to such a miserable end.

Well, *almost* nobody. We know how Jesus did that. He declared that no one took his life from Him. Rather He laid it down of His own will. We understand the purpose of redemption being purchased for us by the sacrifice of Jesus there.

But Paul spoke of the cross as the only place where he would glory, and that because he said the world had been crucified to him and he to the world at the cross of Jesus. Who would gladly give up all Paul had sacrificed in order to be where Paul was when he wrote this letter to the Galatians? Who would glory in being persecuted, slandered, placed under economic hardship? It all happened because of the cross for Paul, and he gloried in it!

What do we boast in?

19. DO YOU WANT TO BE MADE WELL?

"When Jesus saw him lying there, and knew that he already had been in that condition a long time, He said to Him, 'Do you want to be made well?'" John 5:6.

At the edge of the Pool of Bethesda was a large group of people hoping to be healed by a fabled "troubling of the waters." Naturally, it was only the first one in the pool who was expected to be healed. That didn't include someone seriously ill like this lame man. Perhaps that's why Jesus had compassion on him, seeing his plight and knowing he had been vainly hoping in the legendary "troubling of the waters" when the healing properties of the pool were supposedly released.

So, the question almost causes us to wonder at Jesus' even asking it: "Do you want to be made well?"

Who wouldn't want to be made well? It seems like a question that doesn't make sense. But in view of the fact that a crowd constantly surrounded this pool, and people who were "healed" were probably made well from minor ailments like joint pain or a hang nail makes it apparent they were hoping in odds as farfetched as winning the lottery.

A lot of us are more comfortable having circumstances on which to blame our problems. That way, we're not responsible. Everyone else beats us to the pool when the waters are stirred. We have an excuse to quit looking, to quit trying to change what's wrong. We would rather beg than work for a living. If there's something we're responsible for, then there's something we could do/should do.

The lame man may have had problems that were his own making. We aren't told. He may have been comfortable begging for his sustenance. Being made well would obligate him to work for a living.

Take inventory of yourself with this question: Do you want to be made well? The promise of wholeness, of forgiveness of sins, of a calling to live a holy and godly life is ours, if we really want it. The issue is we must respond to the Savior's invitation positively and take up our mat and go to the employment agency.

20. THE BELOVED LAMB

"The animals that you choose must be year-old males without defect" (Exodus 12:5a)

I once toured the model of the tabernacle of Israel when I visited Eureka Springs, Arkansas. One thing the guide said as he showed us the altar of burnt offering stayed with me. The head of the household was to take his lamb for the Passover to be examined by the priest, and the priest's examination began with this question:

"Do you love this lamb?"

We know the proper answer to that question, don't we? God loved His Only Begotten. Three times while Jesus was on earth, the Gospels record how the Father in heaven boomed His approval of His Son with a loud, heavenly voice – perhaps something comparable to "That's my boy!"

The Father loved His Lamb.

The Lamb was examined by the High Priest who found He claimed to be the Christ. He was examined then by Pilate who declared "I find no fault in this man!"

We can find plenty of fault in ourselves. But the other art of our self-examination around the Table of the Lord should include that discerning question: "Do you love this Lamb?

21. EXAMINE YOURSELVES!

"Examine yourselves to see whether you are in the faith; test yourselves" (II Corinthians 13:5a)

The New Testament includes two of what appear to be three letters Paul has written to the Christians in Corinth. This letter precedes his third (and probably final) visit. Paul's first letter covered a host of problems afflicting this young church in a very pagan environment. Understandably, he covered a broad spectrum of subjects, and told them he had to deal with them as children. This time he wants to be encouraged by how much his "children" have grown since he last saw them.

Part of the Lord's Supper is a period of self-examination. If you think about it, it's that part that looks forward to the Coming Again of our Savior. Just as Paul wanted to find the Corinthians better established and matured in their faith when he returns, the Lord wants to find His servants watching faithfully, doing His will, having made the most of the time allotted to them.

Examine yourselves.

22. GOD WILL PROVIDE HIMSELF

"And Abraham said, My son, God will provide himself a lamb for a burnt offering" (Genesis 22:8 [KJV])

Oftentimes the King James Version says it in the most memorable form, even if it seems a bit awkward for conventional English. The wording of the text just presented is familiar in context. Abraham was ascending Mt. Moriah with Isaac to obey the command of the Lord to offer his son to Him as a burnt offering. By this point in his life, Isaac was a stropping teenager, quite capable of figuring out some of the irregularities in this journey, the coals and wood for the fire, and the absence of the animal for sacrifice. Maybe he even detected a tremor in his father's voice when Abraham told the servants "Stay here with the donkey, and the young man and I will go up there to worship. Afterwards, we both will come back to you."

Whatever the reason, Isaac's question was from more than childish innocence; and his father's reply was from an unwavering faith that steadied Isaac's steps up the hill. "God will provide Himself the lamb for the burnt offering."

Abraham didn't waver, and Isaac didn't resist. At the last second, Abraham's knife hand was stayed from plunging the fatal blow. God provided a ram in the thicket, and Abraham and Isaac both returned to the servants, just as he said.

The name of the place of "Yahweh Yireh" (The Lord Will Provide). Jewish tradition says it was the future site of the Temple, Mt. Moriah. But the Temple was originally built on a ridge, rather than a peak. When stones were quarried to rebuild the wall and the Temple after the captivity, they were cut from the center of the ridge, leaving the Temple on one side within the city and another part of the mountain outside of the city walls.

It was on this hill outside the city our Lord was crucified, the perfect Lamb of God Who took away the sins of the world. Indeed, as He had done centuries earlier on the same mountain, God provided Himself the Lamb.

23. DEATH AND TAXES

"Just as people are destined to die once, and after that to face judgment, so Christ was sacrificed once to take away the sins of man; and he will appear a second time, not to bear sin, but to bring salvation to those who are waiting for him (Heb. 9:27, 28)

"Nothing is as certain as death and taxes," is a quote attributed to Ben Franklin. It's been repeated often, but you have to wonder about the accuracy. Some people evade taxes and get room and meals in prison paid by those who pay taxes! And if you are alive when the Lord returns, you might miss out on the physical death experienced by all generations preceding that final one.

Alive when Christ returns or not, we will all face judgment! It is more certain than death and taxes put together.

It was the certainty that all human beings will face judgment that made the death of Jesus certain. Someone had to pay the penalty incurred by human beings in their fallen estate. As certain as judgment, the death of Jesus was inevitable. The combination of God's justice and love put the plan for our redemption in motion from the very beginning.

When Jesus first came, it was to face death on our behalf. When Jesus comes again, all will face judgment; but the text we read says the real reason for His Second Appearance is to bring salvation to all who keep this vigil until He comes.

24. SEEING GOD'S FACE IN MY ENEMY

"'No, please!' said Jacob. 'If I have found favor in your eyes, accept this gift from me. For to see your face is like seeing the face of God, now that you have received me favorably.'" (Genesis33:10).

The night before Jacob encountered Esau, he had prayed to the Lord to deliver him from the hand of his brother. The last time Jacob had seen Esau, his twin brother had vowed to kill him. Now, twenty years later, Esau was coming to meet Jacob with seven hundred men.

This wasn't the Welcome Wagon!

Besides prayer, Jacob had sent a long retinue of gifts ahead of him. When they met, the once estranged brothers embraced and wept. Esau at first tried to refuse the lavish gifts of Jacob, but in our text we read how Jacob insisted. He said seeing Esau's face favorably was like seeing the face of God.

I remember one particular First Day assembly where two Japanese guests sat beside a Filipino who once had sworn he would kill any Japanese he saw because of all the horrors he had experienced in Manila during World War II. Reconciliation is the business of the cross. Our God reconciles us to Him. He reconciles us with each other in the same way. To be received favorably by a former enemy is possible only where grace and mercy are the predominant themes.

The Lord's Table is a great place to assess those relationships we might be able to heal, the ones we have wronged hearing our apologies, the ones who have wronged us receiving our forgiveness. If God can reconcile us to Him, we certainly ought to be able to reconcile with one another.

Or, as Jacob put it to Esau: "To see your face is like seeing the face of God, now that you have received me favorably."

25. BUT GOD INTENDED IT FOR GOOD

"You intended to harm me, but God intended it for good to accomplish what is now being done, the saving of many lives" (Genesis 50:20).

As he had dreamed years earlier, Joseph's brothers were again prostrate before him. They feared, now that their father was dead, he would exact retribution upon them. After all, they knew they deserved it!

Once again, Joseph wept and freely forgave. He saw the eternal plan at this point. This deed which had been so wrong on his brothers' part was a plan in God's mind to save the entire nation to come from Israel. Joseph's brothers, at their very worst, had actually helped to accomplish God's plans.

The story of Joseph foreshadowed the Gospel. Those who crucified the Lord of Glory committed the foulest deed of all history. Yet the Man of Sorrows prayed forgiveness even as He was crucified. They intended to harm Him, but God intended it for good, the saving of many lives. Even now, when guilty people come before Him and plead for His mercy, they find He freely forgives and comforts. What we once meant for rebellion is forgotten, and we are welcomed as family.

26. THE CROSS BEARING CHALLENGE

"If anyone would come after me, he must deny himself and take up his cross and follow me" (Matthew 16:24).

A few years ago on Facebook, several people (perhaps even you) took "The Ice Bucket Challenge" to fund research for ALS – Lou Gehrig's Disease. The person would accept the challenge from someone else to make a contribution to the ALS Research Foundation and then would do a video of himself/herself dumping a bucket of ice water over the head and challenging all Facebook friends to make a contribution and pass the challenge on in similar fashion.

After Peter said something so right Jesus said the Father in Heaven had revealed it to him, Peter then contradicted Jesus' prediction that He would be arrested and abused and ultimately killed in Jerusalem. To this, Jesus rebuked Peter by telling Satan to get behind Him.

The Cross was inevitable for Jesus. His work of redemption depended upon the Cross. To set all of His disciples straight on this, Jesus then turned to all His disciples and issued the Cross Challenge. He was going to His Cross in response to the challenge of sinful mankind. He then turned to His disciples and said, "If you follow in my footsteps, you will take up *your* cross and follow me!

His disciples understood it better then than we do today. We see crosses atop church buildings and chapels. They saw crosses along the roadways leading into town. We bear crosses in gold chains around our necks. They bore crosses on their shoulders as they marched to certain death. The Cross Challenge was far from a fad. Jesus was *dead serious* when He laid it down.

History records that the Twelve picked up the challenge. Except for Judas, they all suffered, to the man, for the cause of the Gospel of Jesus Christ. Twelve died martyrs' deaths. The one who didn't, died an exiled prisoner.

27. ONCE "NOT MY PEOPLE"

"Once you were not a people, but now you are the people of God; once you had not received mercy, but now you have received mercy" (I Peter 2:10).

Did you ever hear people laughing at an "inside joke"? It's like you don't have the "decoder ring" everybody else is using. That can also go with cryptic references only the insiders get.

This text from I Peter 2:10 can be appreciated only by those familiar with the Old Testament prophets. Hosea was the prophet who was commanded by the Lord to marry a prostitute as a way of showing how God's relationship with Israel was strained by Israel's infidelity to Him. Hosea's wife bore him three children: Jezreel (a reference to the violence of king Jehu), Lo-ruhama (no mercy), and Lo-ammi (not my people). Peter says that was our plight before Christ redeemed us. We were not a people with any significant identity, but now we are the children of God. We had been without mercy from anyone, but now we have obtained God's mercy.

More important than being an insider on a joke or some cryptic reference is being an insider on the loving kindness of the Lord God. Though once we had been unfaithful and undeserving, now He has accepted us. Through Jesus, we have at last been included!

28. TAKE A LOOK

"In the year that King Uzziah died, I saw…" (Isaiah 6:1a).

Here near the beginning of his book, the prophet Isaiah explains what motivates him. He describes when the Lord called him to his prophetic ministry. It was a moving, memorable experience.

He looked and saw the Lord, high and lifted up. His train filled the Temple, where Isaiah had his vision. Even the seraphs ministering to Him were impressive. All Isaiah could say of his plight was, "Woe is me, for I am undone!" Ordinary men don't just "look at God." God told Moses nobody could see His face and live. The seraphs who ministered in the Lord's presence had wings to cover their feet and faces in the presence of God.

He looked and saw himself. Isaiah knew how sinful he was. He lived in a sinful nation. He had no illusions about his standing when he already had seen the God Who was "Holy! Holy! Holy!" He was desperately in need of cleansing. In response to this need, one of the angelic beings touched a coal from the altar to Isaiah's lips. He was cleansed.

He looked and saw the calling of God. When the voice from the Throne thundered, "Whom shall I send? Who will go for me?" it was only logical that Isaiah respond, "Here am I; send me." He had been cleansed especially for this task. God had appeared to him for this very reason.

Take a look at God – high and lifted up. Take a look at yourself, sinful, but now cleansed. Take a look at the Lord's calling to you.

Will you likewise respond, "Here am I; send me!"

29. MORE THAN YOU COULD IMAGINE!

"Now to him who is able to do immeasurably more than all we ask or imagine, according to the power that is at work within us, to him be glory in the church and in Christ Jesus throughout all generations, for ever and ever! Amen. (Ephesians 3:20, 21).

When Luke Skywalker was trying to persuade Han Solo to rescue Princess Leia, he said, "She could make you rich!"

"How rich?" asked Solo.

"More than you could imagine!"

To which Solo replied, "I've got a pretty active imagination, kid!"

Paul closes this section of his letter to the Ephesians with this doxology. He is able to do above all that we ask or think – more than we could imagine! What's more, He does it through the power at work within us, His Holy Spirit.

News flashes about people who have lifted fallen cars off of loved ones come to mind. Some experts have called it "hysteric strength." Adrenaline kicks in, and they accomplish something they never imagined possible within themselves.

Even without adrenaline, God's people are capable of still more! Read Hebrews 11, and see what has been accomplished by the past heroes of faith. Realize that we are running our event now, while those who have gone on before are in the stands, cheering us on.

How big is your imagination?

God is even bigger!

30. BURIED/RISEN WITH CHRIST

"And you have been given fullness in Christ,…having been buried with him in baptism and raised with him through your faith in the power of God, who raised him from the dead" (Colossians 2:10, 12).

When Christians speak of "being like Jesus" as their greatest aspiration, they need to return to the beginning of their walk – baptism into Jesus Christ. According to Romans 6:1-6, baptism into Christ is the reenactment of the death, burial, and resurrection of our Lord.

A believer dies to sin. He closes his eyes. He stops breathing. He is passive, doing no work of his own.

The believer is buried, put into a cold tomb.

He is then raised up out of the tomb and opens his eyes on a new world. He is now a new creation in Christ, no longer controlled by sin.

More than simply a singular point of history, this event is also to be the turning point in our personal lives. We should behave like new people. We should have a totally new perspective. God has given us the full measure of Christ when we identified with Him in baptism. What we do with that full measure in us is still ours to decide.

Do we really want to be like Jesus? Then we are expected to act like it.

31. BEFORE WORSHIP

"Therefore if you bring your gift to the altar, and there remember that your brother has something against you, leave your gift there before the altar, and go your way. First be reconciled to your brother, and then come offer your gift" (Matthew 5:23, 24).

Formal acts of worship have their purpose and their place, but they will never outshine genuine religion. It's one thing to sing songs about how much we love the Lord. It's more important to give up the secret sins that keep us apart from Him.

Likewise, Jesus spoke about the priority of being reconciled to one another before we bring our gift to the altar for liturgical worship. Reconciliation to God is the centerpiece of the Gospel. God was in Christ Jesus, reconciling a world of sinners to Himself. Our being reconciled to God is why we take the name of Jesus to ourselves and commit to be His exclusively.

But John asks a common sense question: How can someone claim to love God, whom he hasn't seen, while he hates his brother whom he has seen? It is in this context that Jesus warns us about making things right with one another. It's more important that formal worship.

Here, at the assembly, we come to the Lord's Table and recommit our lives to the One Who gave all for us. But what if something stands between us and someone else – something we could make right? Jesus says it's more important to be reconciled with our brother than to offer our gift formally at the altar.

That doesn't mean a herd of people should get up and go, right now; but it does mean there is something even more important than observing the Lord's Supper. We need to give it such priority that the sun won't set on our anger tonight.

32. THE LIFE WITHOUT CHRIST

"As for you, you were dead in your transgressions and sins in which you used to live when you followed the ways of this world and of the ruler of the kingdom of the air, the spirit who is now at work in those who are disobedient" (Ephesians 2:1, 2).

Back in the late 1970's television witnessed nostalgia for the 1950's with the show "Happy Days."

Those who lived in the 1950's with good recollection recognize some differences. Polio killed and crippled people. The Iron Curtain went up in Europe. Kids had "duck and cover" exercises in school. Guys like Fonzie weren't so lovable; they stole hubcaps and carried switchblades. The "Happy Days" weren't really that happy!

When the wandering Israelites complained to Moses in the wilderness, the most common complaint was about "the good old days" back in Egypt. They remembered leeks, onions, and cucumbers. Their "selective amnesia" forgot the sting of the taskmaster's whip and the order to make more bricks with less straw.

The phenomenon about the "good old days" is that the older they get, the "gooder" they seem to be!

For this reason, Paul's description of all the wonderful things God has done for us is joined with this reminder about what the believer's former life was like:

We were dead in our transgressions.

We were commanded by Satan and led by the passions He provoked in us.

We were objects of God's wrath, separate from Christ, excluded from Israel.

We were without hope, without God.

We need to remember that the "good old days" are old, but they certainly weren't good! Our situation was so desperate that it took the death of Christ on our behalf to bring us out.

33. A TALE OF TWO GOATS

"When Aaron has finished making atonement for the Most Holy Place, the Tent of Meeting and the altar, he shall bring forward the live goat. He is to lay both hands on the head of the live goat and confess over it all the wickedness and rebellion of the Israelites – all their sins – and put them on the goat's head. He shall send the goat away into the desert in the care of a man appointed for the task" (Leviticus 16:20, 21)

These two goats which were offered up on the Day of Atonement each year are interesting. One was killed, and its blood was put on the horns of the other. The other was led into the desert with the sins of the people laid upon it through the blood placed on it.

We are familiar with the Blood Atonement sacrifice of Jesus on our behalf, but what are we to do with the type of the scapegoat in Leviticus 16? This is the living goat with the blood applied to it.

The Blood of Christ has been applied to us. We are called upon to be living sacrifices (Romans 12:1). Our sins are paid for, but we are to bear the sins of others as we are led into the wilderness, susceptible to the elements of a hostile world. This is the Great Commission to the Lord's church. With the Gospel in our hearts and on our lips, we become agents of forgiveness of sins to the dying world around us.

As Jesus willingly accepted His death for the payment of the sins of the world, may we also willingly accept our calling to bear the reproaches of others for the redemption of the lost around us!

34. KISS THE SON

"Kiss the Son, lest he be angry
  and you be destroyed in your way,
for his wrath can flare up in a moment.
Blessed are all who take refuge in him" (Psalm 2:12).

I Kings 1 tells us how Adonijah had tried to establish the throne of David to himself, while his father was still alive and old. David had already promised the throne to Solomon, but Adonijah had enlisted the support of some rather impressive names – Joab, the field commander of the military; Abiathar, the High Priest; and several other nobles.

Nathan the Prophet gave Bathsheba a heads up. After all, if Adonijah succeeded in setting himself up as king, she and Solomon would most certainly be put to death. Nathan had Bathsheba inquire of David about what was going on, and he timed it so he would come in just as David would be seeking verification.

Once David was convinced Adonijah was preparing to steal the throne, he immediately had the coronation of Solomon carried out. He had Zadok, the Priest do the anointing. Solomon was paraded through Jerusalem on a royal mount, and seated on the royal throne. The people celebrated loudly.

As quickly as word reached Adonijah's illegitimate coronation feast, everybody decided the party was over and went home quickly and quietly. Solomon had been crowned king over Israel at the word of David himself.

Psalm 2 is both a Messianic Psalm and a reflection on this bit of intrigue from Israel's history. Those nobles who swore fealty to the new king signified their allegiance by kissing him. Those who hadn't already thrown in with Adonijah were quick to kiss the son David had seated on his throne. Adonijah, Joab, and Abiathar lost their prestigious roles.

We have been on the wrong side too long in this conflict. The legitimate King extends His royal hand toward us. It is time to kiss the Son, before we find ourselves forever His enemy.

35. KICKING AGAINST THE GOADS

"We all fell to the ground, and I heard a voice saying to me in Aramaic, 'Saul, Saul, why do you persecute me? It is hard for you to kick against the goads'" (Acts 26:14b)

The rebuke of Jesus to the persecutor of early Christians had its own observation. Persecute the believers, and you persecute Jesus. The more you resist, the harder it becomes. Stephen's arguments had been perfect. Saul couldn't refute them. The more he chased the believers across the countryside, the more they disseminated the Gospel. As sincere as his efforts had been to his Pharisaical tradition, everything came unraveled. Now, the very One he denied was the Messiah appeared to him in resplendent glory.

He was like an ox rebelling against the goad stuck in his haunches only to get hurt all the more when he kicked it. This was a humiliating experience.

Yielding to the Lord has always been painful and humiliating. Pride is what led us away in our rebellion against the Lord. Swallowing our pride leaves a bitter taste in the mouth, but kicking against the goads hurts even more and gains nothing new. In compassion, the Lord appears to us and gently rebukes us: "It's hard to kick against the goads!"

Quit kicking. Swallow the pride. Yield to the Messiah.

36. CAN THESE BONES LIVE?

"The hand of the Lord was upon me, and he brought me out by the Spirit of the Lord and set me in the middle of a valley; it was full of bones.... He asked me, 'Son of man, can these bones live'
I said, 'O Sovereign Lord, you alone know'" (Ezekiel 37:1, 3).

In World War II, the Army Ordnance Department adopted the slogan, "The difficult we do immediately; the impossible takes a little longer." It summarized the "can do" attitude of the greatest generation of Americans that led to victory.

But the more common slogan for Americans today is "That's above my pay grade!"

Welcome to the realm of things you cannot do! Look honestly, and the list of things we cannot do certainly runs much longer than the list of things we can do. And at the top of the list is the matter of raising the dead.

Ezekiel was inspired by the Holy Spirit when he was given the vision of the valley of the bones and was asked whether or not these bones could come to life. His reply shows the divine wisdom needed to answer God's question: "O Sovereign Lord, you alone know."

It wasn't up to Ezekiel. Only God can raise the dead. Those bones would come to life only if the Lord wanted them to come to life.

This vision was prophetic of the restoration of the exiled nation of Israel, but it clearly applies to a world of spiritually dead humans. They are dried bones, hopelessly dead. They are powerless to change their status.

Can you call these bones to life again, Ezekiel?

"That's above my pay grade!"

But God had Ezekiel prophesy to them, and by the power of God through the word spoken by Ezekiel, the scattered bones came together. Flesh appeared on them and embodied them again. At a further word spoken by Ezekiel at the Lord's command, the breath of life entered the bodies, and the dead lived again!

To participate in the Gospel of Jesus Christ is to share in the miraculous power of God to raise the dead. May God's children be filled with the Spirit and speak as the Lord has commanded!

37. DIE FOR A DOG?

"You see, at just the right time, when we were still powerless, Christ died for the ungodly. Very rarely will anyone die for a righteous man, though for a good man someone might possibly dare to die. But God demonstrates his own love for us in this: While we were still sinners, Christ died for us" (Romans 5:6-8).

Several years ago, I heard about a house fire where the entire family made it outside safely, but the dog was still inside. A boy in the family named Eric ran back into the burning building to rescue his dog, and Eric perished. As reporters published the story, they quoted Eric's father as saying, "Eric loved that dog so much it cost him his life."

Don't underestimate the power of love, even for a simple family pet. The difference between the Sovereign God and His creatures is even greater than the difference between a boy and his dog. Yet that didn't keep the Lord from dying for His creatures. He did this while we were *sinful* creatures. He gave us redemption not because we deserved it, but because we needed it.

Like Eric, the Lord loved us so much it cost Him his life.

38. I AM THE GATE

"I am the gate; whoever enters through me will be saved" (John 10:9)

Right in the middle of a profound allegory of being the Good Shepherd who lays down his life for the sheep, Jesus makes this declaration about being the gate. Is He mixing metaphors?

Sheep corrals weren't the same thing then that we envision. No wire, obviously – but they weren't wood either. The corrals were fashioned by thorn bushes and brambles woven into tight masses about neck high all around. A small opening about three or four feet wide was left for the sheep to enter and leave.

So how do you hang a gate on brambles and briars? Shepherds back then didn't. They brought the sheep out of pasture into the safety of the corral and counted them as they entered. Once the herd was fully gathered, the shepherd would lie down across the opening. Sheep could not get out, and wolves and thieves could not get in without going over the shepherd.

If the sheep couldn't be harmed without the shepherd being removed, Jesus was declaring that His sheep would be harmed only "over His dead body"! That's exactly how the story of redemption was carried out. The enemy killed Messiah, hoping for access to the sheep. But Messiah is still there, guarding the corral, and denying entry to any other than His sheep.

39. THE TRUE COLOR OF SIN

"Come now, let us reason together," says the Lord.
"Though you sins are like scarlet, they shall be as white as snow;
Though they be red like crimson, they shall be as wool" (Isaiah
1:18).

Before digital photography, the big name was Kodak. One of
their commercials had a beautiful jingle, where singers said, "I see
your true colors shining through." Their products showed brilliant
colors with original clarity

What's the true color of sin? Most poets and artists depict it as
darkness and black.

The Bible, however doesn't speak of sin as black. It
consistently speaks of sin as blood-red. The color of sin is crimson.

This imagery should stir our minds and hearts even more.
Blood was life. Sin meant death. The price of sin was always the
shedding of blood. Hebrew worshippers offered a blood offering for
their sins. Jesus poured out His blood for our sins.

Sin is awful – far worse than total darkness! It required the
perfect Son of God in payment for what we have done. We can't
minimize how offensive sin is to the Holy and Just God. Someone
had to pay what sin demands in death. Jesus freely paid it. It was an
awful, bloody red!

On the Cross Jesus revealed our true colors, shining through.

40. THE SNAKE ON THE POLE

"Just as Moses lifted up the snake in the desert, so the Son of Man must be lifted up, that everyone who believes in him may have eternal life" (John 3:14, 15)

Just before the most popularly quoted Scripture verse among Christians (John 3:16) Jesus referenced an event from the wilderness wanderings found in Numbers. The Israelites had been grumbling and complaining against God, against Moses, against the taste of manna. They learned to grumble so fluently it had become their native language!

In punishment for their grumbling on one occasion, God sent serpents with a fiery, deadly bite for which there was no antidote. Once again, God captured their attention away from whatever their grumbling was about. When they cried for mercy, God had Moses establish an antidote – a bronze snake, lifted up on a pole in the middle of the camp. To be cured of the deadly snake bite, the victim had only to look upon the bronze snake.

Jesus alluded to the snake on the pole in his conversation with Nicodemus. He said it was a type of what was to happen to Him. Moses lifted up the snake on the pole so that the Israelites could be saved from an awful death. In Jesus, the Serpent of Eden would be lifted up on a pole so that all who looked upon the Son of Man in faith could be saved from eternal death.

Eternal life can be ours for looking at the Christ of the cross. Apparently, there were some who refused to look on the bronze snake on the pole in the wilderness. They were the ones who "tested God in the wilderness" (I Corinthians 10:9) and were killed.

Never be ashamed to look upon the Christ of the cross! There is eternal life to be gained for all who look there for life. There is nothing but death for those who turn away.

41. FINDING FAVOR

"But Noah found favor in the eyes of the Lord" (Genesis 6:8).

In view that the Lord utterly destroyed everything outside of the ark in the world that existed before the Flood, the simple statement of Genesis 6:8 says a great deal! The end of all flesh had come into the mind of the Lord. Everything was corrupt, and the thoughts of all people were only evil constantly.

Noah had his sins too. Despite those faults, the Lord hadn't given up on him and his family. Noah was willing to obey the word of the Lord that came to him and by faith built the ark in preparation for the Flood. Faith was the avenue of God's favor. Because Noah believed God, he obeyed God. Because Noah believed and obeyed God, he found favor in the eyes of the Lord.

The Lord will judge the world again, this time by fire. The Lord has provided an ark for the preservation of people who trust in Him. It is the Cross of Jesus Christ. As Noah and has family entered the ark, we flee to Jesus for protection.

May we all find favor in God's eyes before He judges the world again.

42. MUCH MORE THAN THAT

"Amaziah asked the man of God, 'But what about the hundred talents I paid for these Israelite troops?'

"The man of God replied, 'The Lord can give you much more than that'' (II Chronicles 25:9).

Amaziah had hired mercenaries to help him in battle. They were soldiers from the Northern Kingdom, which had given itself to idolatry. It had cost him about three quarters of a ton of silver to enlist a hundred thousand additional soldiers to help fight against Syria.

God sent a prophet to rebuke Amaziah. Amaziah had trusted the Lord in the past and been delivered. What he needed to do now was to trust the Lord again.

A practical question came to mind: What about the hundred talents of silver he had paid the soldiers from the Northern Kingdom? That was a lot of money!

A lesson in trust came in the reply, "The Lord can give you much more than that." Amaziah realized victory without the mercenaries.

Jesus told a pair of brief parables back to back. They were both about men who gave up everything to gain a field with a hidden treasure and a singular pearl of great price, respectively. The focus wasn't upon what they gave up, though what they gave up was an essential part of the stories. The focus was on what they gained for the trade.

Too often, we can't trust the Lord enough to let go of what we deem valuable. We need to hear the words of the prophet again: "The Lord can give you much more than that."

43. MAKE IT SO!

"As the rain and the snow come down from heaven,
and do not return to it without watering the earth
and making it bud and flourish,
so that it yields seed for the sower
and bread for the eater,
So is my word that goes out from my mouth:
It will not return to me empty,
but will accomplish what I desire
and achieve the purpose for which I sent it" (Isaiah 55:10-11).

If you ever followed the *Star Trek* series on television or in the motion pictures, you are familiar with Captain Jean Luc Picard from the Next Generation series. One of his most familiar lines is his response to a proposed course of action that he thinks should be done: "Make it so!"

The command reflects authority. As commander of the vessel, he didn't have to repeat the proposal or paraphrase it in his own words. He needed only to command it.

No one speaks with greater authority than God. In the Genesis account of creation we read how God command that different aspects of the world and its inhabitants come into being and be organized. He spoke, "and it was so."

Whenever God speaks, it is so. It happens just as He commanded it to happen. Here in Isaiah 55, God is promising to fulfill His word about better days after judgment on the land. When people turn to Him, He promises to return to them.

I have less authority. Even when I make a promise in good faith there are times things change, and I am powerless to do as I promised. God has no such problems. As surely as creation functions according to the genius of His design, whatever He has spoken will come to pass. God's word will not come back unfulfilled. When all is over, what He has spoken will be!

44. FOR THEM OR FOR US?

"Now when Joshua was near Jericho, he looked up and saw a man standing in front of him with a drawn sword in his hand. Joshua went up to him and asked, 'Are you for us or for our enemies?'

"'Neither,' he replied, 'but as commander of the army of the Lord I have now come.' Then Joshua fell facedown to the ground in reverence…" (Joshua 5:13, 14).

During the Civil War, a reporter asked President Abraham Lincoln if he firmly believed God was on the side of the Union forces. Lincoln wisely replied, "My concern has never been whether or not God was on our side, but rather that we were on His side!"

Joshua was commander of the nation of Israel. So, when he led Israel toward Jericho and he saw a man with a drawn sword he properly approached the swordsman and asked, "Are you for us or for our enemies?"

The answer was, "None of the above!" This swordsman was no simple man. He was the Commander of the Heavenly Host. So he replied, "Neither!" He wasn't a warrior for one side or the other. He was the commander for God's side!

Joshua immediately fell on his face before this commander. He ranked above Joshua. He was not there to take orders from Joshua, great as Joshua was as the leader of Israel. He was there to give orders to Joshua.

Our prayer lives could profit from this example. God and the angels or heaven are not at our beck and call to do what we desire for them to do for us. They are there to accomplish what God desires for us! If our plans and actions conflict with the wishes of God, they need to be surrendered.

May we all fall on our faces before the Commander of the Army of the Lord!

45. OPEN HIS EYES

"When the servant of the man of God got up and went out early the next morning, an army with horses and chariots had surrounded the city (Dothan). 'Oh, my lord, what shall we do?' the servant asked.

"'Don't be afraid,' the prophet answered. 'Those who are with us are more than those who are with them.'

"And Elisha prayed, 'O Lord, open his eyes so he may see.' Then the Lord opened the servant's eyes, and he looked and saw the hills full of horses and chariots of fire all around Elisha" (II Kings 6:15-17).

Perspective will change your frame of mind. Peter saw Jesus walking on the water and was bold enough to say, "If it really is you, let me walk on the water!' As far as we know, he is the only one who dared to ask; and Jesus said, "Come!"

Somewhere, out on the water, Peter's focus changed. Maybe the wind picked up, or an exceptionally large wave came under Peter's feet and lifted him up and settled him down again. Whatever the reason, Peter took his eyes off Jesus and looked more at the waves. Probably, it is an understatement to say, "He began to sink." More likely, it was as if he had been walking the plank, and the plank gave way.

Splash!

"Glug, glug! Lord, save me!" shortest prayer recorded in Scripture.

The servant of Elisha saw only the army of Syria surrounding Dothan. Elisha saw things from the heavenly perspective. The servant worried. Elisha was as cool as a cucumber.

When we focus on the waves about us, and our lives crash; when we see only the enemy forces and have lost sight of the host of heaven surrounding them, we need to pray for an eye opening experience. Those with us are greater than those who are with them!

46. GREAT DESIRE, GREAT EFFORT

"Then He said to them, 'With fervent desire I have desired to eat this Passover with you before I suffer'" (Luke 22:15 [NKJV]).

Whenever we speak of the Final Week in Jesus' life, we often hear the term "Passion" with it. The one time Jesus used a term which speaks of a passionate desire is here, at the Passover table before His arrest. The word used in Greek is the same word translated "lust" in a negative context. Here, and also in reference to a man who *desires* to do the work of an Overseer, it speaks positively of what the person's Passion is.

As he was dying of a crippling neurological disease, David E. Ireland wrote a series of letters to the child he would never see. Mind you, his wife was pregnant with the child when he wrote the following:

"Your mother is very special. Few men know what it's like to receive appreciation for taking their wives out to dinner when it entails what it does for us. It means that she has to dress me, shave me, brush my teeth, comb my hair; wheel me out of the house and down the steps, open the garage and put me in the car, take the pedals off the chair, stand me up, sit me in the seat of the car, twist me around so that I'm comfortable, fold the wheelchair, put it in the car, go around to the other side of the car, start it up, back it out, get out of the car, pull the garage door down, get back into the car, and drive off to the restaurant."

Mind you, what she does once, she has to do four times in such an evening, since they arrive at the restaurant and then go home again.

"We sit down to have dinner, and she feeds me throughout the entire meal. And when it's over she pays the bill,... and when it's over – finished – with real warmth she'll say, 'Honey, thank you for taking me out to dinner.' I never quite know how to answer."

This final Passover meal where Jesus established the Memorial we celebrate on the First Day of the week, Jesus spoke of a deep desire to have it with His Disciples. It was as if He were thanking them – thanking us – for having the meal! We never know quite what to say.

We should be thanking Him!

47. THE FELLOWSHIP OF SUFFERING

"…that I may know Him and the power of His resurrection, and the fellowship of His sufferings, being conformed to His death…." (Philippians 3:10[NKJV])

Whenever you hear the word "fellowship" what comes to mind? A church outing? A carry-in dinner? The "meet and greet" period in morning worship? We do know that the early church continued steadfastly in the Apostles' teaching, in the breaking of bread, in fellowship, and in prayer, but what do we really mean when we use that word "fellowship."

The original word in the original language was *KOINONIA*. It meant "to have in common." When we share common interests, common goals, and common experiences we are fellowshipping.

Paul aspired to know Christ as fully as possible. He wanted to be conformed to the likeness of Christ and ultimately follow in His resurrection to eternal life.

Part of his aspirations meant knowing "the fellowship of His sufferings." Jesus had shared our griefs and sorrows. Paul wanted to share with Jesus in His suffering.

When we consider all that Jesus suffered on our behalf, how often are we motivated to have His sufferings in common with our own experience? This was a far cry from a carry-in dinner or weeknight get together! This was an intimate knowledge of the Savior Who was known as "a Man of sorrows, familiar with grief."

May we all desire to know Christ so fully that we even accept a call to share in His sufferings!

48. MERCY OVER LITURGY

"If you had known what these words mean, 'I desire mercy, not sacrifice,' you would not have condemned the innocent" (Matthew 12:7).

When Jesus' critics sought to get to Him by picking on His disciples for plucking grains from the edge of a field and chewing on them on the Sabbath, Jesus replied with several arguments, including the fact that David and his men ate sacred loaves from the table of the showbread under special circumstances.

The real clincher, though, was Jesus' quote from Micah 6:6. "I desire mercy, not sacrifice." While legalists were holding to tradition that would forbid the smallest semblance of labor on the Sabbath (harvesting and winnowing) on the part of His disciples, Jesus pointed out a greater issue. How about mercy? God had prioritized it over formal worship (sacrifice).

The critics singled out Jesus' disciples because of their association with Him. They were hyper-critical of this action, which from the surface was innocent and harmless. This wasn't really harvesting and winnowing any more than unwrapping a sandwich is food preparation! In their hatred for Jesus, they grumbled about this action and condemned innocent people.

Are we for mercy? The merciful obtain mercy. Do we condemn non-Christians for doing unchristian things? Do we insist others hold to our traditions which, while helpful to structure our own Christian walk, are not really required in Scripture? People really don't care how much you know until they know how much you care.

May we give mercy the priority the Lord gives to it!

49. THE MARK OF A PROTECTED HOUSEHOLD

"Then they are to take some of the blood and put in on the sides and tops of the doorframes of the houses where they eat the lambs" (Exodus 12:7)

God has His reasons for everything He commands. It takes very little imagination to understand how the sprinkling of the blood of the Paschal lamb on the doorposts of the house foreshadowed the shedding of the blood of Jesus on the Cross. The blood was sprinkled at the head and the side pillars, so that the sign of the cross was made in the very action.

Perhaps something less obvious is the fact that this was the mark of household which would be protected from death. The Blood of the Lamb protects households!

When parents partake of the emblems of the Lord's Supper, their children recognize it is a special event in their parents' lives. The questions the children ask present the "teachable moments" important to the spiritual education and development of their children. Even though the decision to follow Christ will ultimately be their own, the children will at least know about Jesus, His death, and following Him so they can make an informed decision.

"Believe on the Lord Jesus Christ," Paul told the Philippian jailor in Acts 16, "and you will be saved – you and your household." Our decision to follow Jesus is not made in a vacuum. It affects those around us as well. Children observe this memorial feast, and it educates them in a positive way.

50. WEARY OF LABOR? COME TO WORK!

"Come to me, all you who are weary and burdened, and I will give you rest. Take my yoke upon you and learn from me, for I am gentle and humble in heart, and you will find rest for your souls. For my yoke is easy and my burden is light" (Matthew 11:28-30)

Motivational speaker Zig Ziglar said, "If you want to be happy at work, find something you really like to do; you'll never work another day in your life!"

I can't help but think of that one-liner anytime I read the Great Invitation given by Jesus in the passage just cited. Jesus extends His invitation to all who are exhausted and overworked. He promises them rest. But His solution isn't taking an extended vacation!

Instead, He speaks of taking His yoke upon ourselves. A yoke is what an ox or donkey would wear in order to pull a plow. Taking on a yoke sounds like labor, not rest, to me. Doesn't it seem that way to you?

But Jesus said His yoke "is easy." An uneasy yoke didn't bear the burden evenly around the neck and shoulders. It chafed the skin and produced bruises where undue pressure was felt. A good carpenter knew how to work wood and leather in such a way that a yoke fit properly, so it was said to be "easy."

Though He was meek and lowly in heart, there must've been some measure of professional pride in this Nazarene Carpenter when He said His yoke was easy and His burden was light. He guarantees us that if we wear His yoke and enter into labor for Him, it will be well suited for us and not chafe us around the shoulders.

This is work we were made to do! This is what we will truly enjoy doing! Work for Jesus, and you'll never work another day in your life!

51. DEPART A DIFFERENT WAY!

"When the people of the land come before the LORD at the appointed festivals, whoever enters by the north gate to worship is to go out the south gate; and whoever enters by the south gate is to go out the north gate. No one is to return through the gate by which they entered, but each is to go out the opposite gate" (Ezekiel 46:9).

It was that infamous First Day of the week that comes early in the spring once every year – that day when everybody moves his clock ahead one hour to go onto Daylight Saving time. We all lose an hour of sleep that Saturday night, unless we do as some people and forget to move our clocks ahead. In that case, we come in an hour late; and everybody is finishing up what we just intended to start! One such "latecomer" came in the door just as the preacher was bidding everybody good-bye , and she exclaimed, "Oh no! I missed the service!"

"No you didn't," the preacher wisely replied. "The service is just starting."

As the Lord showed Ezekiel the prophet the glory of a new kingdom and a new Temple, He gave an interesting instruction about all who came into the Temple to worship. Whoever came in by the north gate was to leave through the south gate. Whoever came by the south gate was to leave by the north. Every worshipper was to leave a different way than the way by which he came.

It's not hard to catch the symbolism intended in this command. Our worship of the Lord God is supposed to change us. We don't leave the same people we were when first we entered. In fact, it would be wrong to go into the presence of the Lord without expecting it to change us. We enter to worship, but we depart to serve.

52. ACCESS TO GOD

"Having therefore, brethren, boldness to enter into the holiest by the blood of Jesus, By a new and living way, which he hath consecrated for us, through the veil, that is to say, his flesh; And having an high priest over the house of God; Let us draw near with a true heart in full assurance of faith, having our hearts sprinkled from an evil conscience, and our bodies washed with pure water." (Heb 10:19-22)

Do you have a direct line with someone "important"? By this, I mean a celebrity in entertainment or sports, or a ranking government official. I met with Mike Pence twice, when he was my Representative. Of course, I was part of a group getting a tour of the Capitol at the time, and it was his aide who took us on the tour. Mike Pence posed for pictures with us for the last ten minutes of the tour. The second time, he came to report to his constituents in our community.

Usually, the more powerful the person, the less access people have to him. That's why celebrities and politicians talk about having "your people calling my people" to set things up. Even though Esther was Queen of Persia, she risked her life by approaching the throne without an invitation, and that was before her husband, the king! It was a privilege indeed to see the royal scepter extended when she appeared.

Yet there's no one more powerful, more important, than the Creator God. He Himself visited us and set up a venue of righteousness whereby we have access to God – whenever we want!

That access was achieved by Jesus Himself experiencing the plight of our humanness and pleasing the Father with His death, which paid in full the penalty of our sins. No more priesthood is required now that our Great High Priest is right there in the Throne Room! Our people don't have to contact His heavenly beings! We enter in the full assurance that the Royal Scepter has already been extended to us!

This memorial feast celebrates the death, burial and resurrection of Jesus. These emblems speak of all the access we could need to approach the Most Powerful One in all the universe.

53. AND YOUR GOD, MY GOD

"Don't urge me to leave you or to turn back from you. Where you go I will go, and where you stay I will stay. Your people will be my people and your God my God" (Ruth 1:16).

The short book of Ruth is a love story, but it is much more. It is a chapter in the genealogy of David – consequently, in the genealogy of Jesus Christ. It tells how a foreigner, a Moabitess, became one of the ancestors mentioned by name in the genealogy of Jesus in Matthew 1. Moabites were descended from Lot, in a shameful incestuous relationship with his daughter. They worshipped their god Chemosh with human sacrifices.

Something had happened to Ruth when she married into Naomi's family. She found Naomi was worth abandoning everything of her past for. She found Naomi's God was the true God, and not like Chemosh. Despite the fact that Naomi had nothing to offer Ruth, Ruth left everything to make Naomi her only family and the God of Israel her God.

There were those who left everything to follow Jesus. The focus wasn't on what they had given up, but on what they gained. And even as the story of Ruth unfolds, we find so much more gained than what she had given up.

Following Jesus is cause for celebration. We gain Him. Whatever we have to let go of to grab hold onto Him, He is clearly worth it!

54. BUSY HERE AND THERE

"While your servant was busy here and there, the man disappeared" (I Kings 20:40).

Ahab was confronted for failing to do a difficult thing that had been commanded him by the Lord. He was to destroy Ben Hadad, the Syrian king the Lord had given into his hand. A prophet had another prophet wound him, bandaged the wound and talked about having a prisoner being given to his charge – a prisoner he was to guard with his very life. "While your servant was busy here and there, the man disappeared."

Ahab said the man's own words judged him. Then, the prophet revealed himself and showed how Ahab had just pronounced sentence upon himself.

We all make excuses for ourselves when we fail the Lord. He confronts us in such a way that we pass judgment on ourselves. Paul told the Corinthians that when we judge ourselves we are not judged by those on the outside. This is why we are told that the frame of mind necessary to partake of the Lord's Table is one of self-examination. No, we haven't been what we should. No, we haven't kept the word of the Lord. We come here unworthy, in need of the grace and mercy that can be found only at the Cross of Jesus. When we judge ourselves unworthy, we partake in a worthy manner!

55. THE WORK OF AARON AND HUR

"And so it was, when Moses held up his hand, that Israel prevailed; and when he let down his hand, Amalek prevailed. But Moses' hands became heavy; so they took a stone and put it under him, and he sat on it. And Aaron and Hur supported his hands, one on one side, and the other on the other side; and his hands were steady until the going down of the sun. So Joshua defeated Amalek and his people with the edge of the sword" (Exodus 17:11-13).

What do you do with your hands when giving a public speech? That's a problem for more than just a few muddling through the business of a public presentation. I grew weary of the television commercials where the spokesperson used two basic gestures – both hands out, then both hands folded in front. When I pointed it out to my wife, she became annoyed at the same thing I'd observed. Couldn't this local advertiser find a few other things to do with her hands?

This is the only time I read in Scripture about a battle being determined by how someone held his hands. The Israelites prevailed in many other battles without someone holding up his hands for the duration of the conflict. Why would it matter here with Moses?

The most important reason given us in Scripture for assembling with one another regularly is so we can encourage one another all the more as we see the day approaching (Hebrews 10:25). We are engaged in serious spiritual conflict, with souls hanging in the balance. Like Moses' hands, we too grow weary during the drawn out struggle. And like Moses, we all need people like Aaron and Hur standing beside us to hold up our hands when we're too tired to maintain the victorious posture we need. Sometimes we may be Joshua, leading the charge on the battlefield. Sometimes we may be Moses, on the hillside determining the outcome of a struggle by our prayer support. Still other times we may be Aaron and Hur, holding up the feeble hands and encouraging the weary not to give up until the day is ended.

May we not flag in the work of Aaron and Hur!

56. FALLEN FROM GRACE

""You who are trying to be justified by the law have been alienated from Christ; you have fallen away from grace" (Galatians 5:4).

While many people appeal to this passage as scriptural evidence that it is possible for a Christian to fall from grace, it matters even more that we pay attention to what Paul's first concern was. The person who tries to gain his right standing before God by keeping rules and being good enough is working against the very centerpiece of the Gospel – God's grace. We can never be good enough!

I saw a tee shirt one time that had the headline: "If I'm okay and you're okay..."

Then it portrayed Jesus suffering on the Cross, and it continued...

"Explain this!"

We don't assemble every First Day of the week to parade how good we are. We gather around the Table of the Lord to remind ourselves how bad we are without the righteousness provided in the death of Jesus Christ on the Cross. If the Lord's Table doesn't direct our hearts in gratitude for what the Lord has done for us that we could never hope to do for ourselves, we are turning our backs on the very reason we bear the name "Christian." We are here because of grace.

57. THANKS FROM THE BOTTOM OF THE SEA

"I cried out to the Lord because of my affliction,
And He answered me.
'Out of the belly of Sheol I cried,
And you heard by voice'" (Jonah 2:2).

I've certainly heard tell of people giving thanks from the bottom of their heart, but the prayer of Jonah was definitely a one of a kind prayer. It came from the bottom of the sea.

Everybody is familiar with the account of Jonah running from God, only to be tossed about in a stormy sea so badly the only solution the distraught mariners could find was to throw the disobedient prophet overboard. The moment they did, the raging sea became calm.

But in the meantime, a couple of things happened underneath the ocean surface. Jonah described sinking to the depths and having giant kelp wrapping around him as he was surely drowning. But then, a giant sea creature prepared by the Lord swallowed him whole. Jonah found himself surviving the ocean depths by living and breathing in the creature's belly.

I doubt it was cozy in that gastro-intestinal maze. It was dark. It was smelly with stomach juices, even if Jonah did find the air he needed to breathe.

But Jonah was surviving, and for this he gave thanks.

He gave thanks because it was certainly more than he deserved. When he told the ship's crew to throw him overboard, Jonah had no expectations of survival. He deserved to perish. He expected to perish. The only good thing he had done in this story so far was to separate himself from the ship and its crew so they wouldn't perish with him.

He gave thanks because it was more than he expected. Grace and mercy come to all of us from God unexpectedly. We expect the hammer to fall. Instead, God blesses us through Jesus Christ and seats us with Him in the heavenly realms. Now, the belly of a whale may be a far cry from heavenly realms, but it was also a far cry from perishing. Jonah was grateful.

Are you at the bottom of the sea? If you're still alive, maybe there's something for which you could/ you should give thanks.

58. YOU ARE WHAT YOU WEAR

"For all of you who were baptized into Christ have clothed yourselves with Christ" (Galatians 3:27).

Few of us follow fashion designers closely, but still fewer wear leisure suits! We all understand the significance of the words, "You are what you wear." Young people recognize this most, perhaps, because they are so peer conscious. Older people aren't exempt from it either. Didn't we all carefully consider just what we would wear today, considering the event we were going to?

Paul told the Galatians that if they were Christians they should be clothed with Christ. All who were baptized into Christ had "clothed themselves with Christ." Just like a tee shirt advertises whatever is printed on it, or just like a woman's fancy hat worn to the Kentucky Derby, we recognize the true statements made in fashion.

Now is a good time for each of us to ask of ourselves, "Am I wearing Christ in such a way that everyone around me can see? When others look at me, do they see Jesus?"

If not, why not? After all, we are what we wear!

59. BE CAREFUL YOU DON'T FALL

"So, if you think you are standing firm, be careful that you don't fall!" (I Corinthians 10:12).

The tragedy of irony is that too often it is tragic! We can't help but note the irony in some last words of people. For instance, there was Major General John Sedgwick, who in rallying his Union troops at the battle of Spotsylvania Court House said, "They couldn't shoot an elephant at this distance!" Some witnesses said he hadn't even fully finished the words "this distance" before a sharpshooter's bullet hit him in the heart.

A preacher, during invitation time stressed the importance of making the most of the opportunity while we have it. As he warned we may not live to hear another invitation, an annoyed young wife wrote the note to her husband, "I think I'll take my chances." The church custodian found the note where they had been sitting that day. He turned it over to the minister, because the minister was dealing with the grieving family of the same young couple who had been killed in a car wreck on the way home that Sunday.

What if our last words proved to be words of defiance, words of refusal, words of hatred, words of pride? The best way to guard against those kinds of last words is to guard what we say!

Be careful right now, if you think you're in good standing; you just might fall!

60. ALLOCUTE!

"Then I acknowledged my sin to you
and did not cover up my iniquity.
I said, 'I will confess
my transgressions to the Lord.'
And you forgave
the guilt of my sin" (Psalm 32:5).

There have been times I have sat in court on behalf of people who needed the support. Those who need the support most were usually guilty of what they had been charged with.

In most cases, the accused agreed to plead guilty to the charge or to a lesser charge with the promise of a reduced sentence for sparing the court the pains of impaneling a jury and listening to arguments, witnesses, etc. Always, when the agreement was made for the accused to plead guilty, the judge required the defendant to "allocute." It's a technical term, and the judge would refer to it when he talked to counsel; but when he addressed the defendant, he would put it in plainer terms: "Before I pass sentence upon you, I want you to tell the court in plain detail exactly what you did!"

The purpose of confession to God is to acknowledge how we failed Him so He doesn't get blamed for failing us. David spoke of trying to conceal his sin without the desired results. It continued to eat away at him. He finally confessed.

Only in the court of our God, we don't get a reduced sentence! When we allocate, we get a commuted sentence. That means the sentence was "moved on." It was moved onto the back of Jesus and paid in full on the Cross.

61. NUMBERING OUR DAYS

""Teach us to number our days,
that we may gain a heart of wisdom" (Psalm 90:12)..

As George Burns was interviewed around his 100th birthday, he quipped, "If I had known I was going to live this long I would've taken better care of myself!" Despite the fact that he lived to be 100, George Burns died young, compared to Moses. Not only did Moses live to the age of 120, he outlived all but two of the generation that followed him. Joshua and Caleb were the oldest men in Israel after Moses. Everyone else was 60 or younger because of the curse placed on them when they failed to go into the Promised Land 40 years earlier.

But now, even Moses was going to die. Shortly after he wrote Psalm 90, he had already been told by the Lord that he would go up Mt. Pisgah, look into the Promised Land, and die. He wrote these words with the keen realization that he was going the way of all flesh.

Only God is truly Eternal. Only He is from Everlasting to Everlasting – without a beginning point and without end. The rest of us? Well, some live longer than others. Some get to 70, or 80, a few even older than that. But ultimately, we all die.

This life is but an exam – a test to determine our eligibility for the life to come. Furthermore, it is a timed test. When the bell sounds, the test is over. We can't watch the clock and count the seconds down before that bell, but most of us can look in the mirror and realize the clock is winding down! Moses says we need to number our days so that we may gain a heart of wisdom.

Our mortality is a central reason we need Jesus and the hope of Eternal Life that only He can offer.

62. PURELY RELIGIOUS

"Pure and undefiled religion before God and the Father is this: to visit orphans and widows in their trouble, and to keep oneself unspotted from the world" (Jas. 1:27, NKJV).

Sometimes truth is so obvious it needs to be spoken plainly so we don't overlook it by assuming we've been there and heard it.

The book of James is an extremely practical book on Christian living. It challenges the sincerity and depth of our faith by asking whether or not we live it out in our daily lives. In the verses just before this text, he likens too many "religious" people of being empty hearers of the Scripture without letting Scripture change their lives. They're like someone looking in the mirror in the morning without combing their hair, washing their face, straightening the crooked tie. What good is Scripture when we don't do anything to correct what it reveals about us?

Boil it down to the description of pure and undefiled religion. It helps the helpless widow and orphan in the midst of their troubles. It keeps our cleansed vessels holy, unspotted by the world, in our service to God.

There's a lot of empty "stuff" done in the name of religion. Let's look carefully in the Word of God to see that what we do makes our Christianity pure and undefiled in the eyes of God.

63. THE DESIRES OF YOUR HEART

"Delight yourself also in the Lord, and He will give you the desires of your heart" (Psalm 37:4).

There are many accounts that tell of a person rubbing a lantern and having a genie come out who promised to grant a wish. Of course, when it's about the genie in the lantern, we know it's just a story. Usually, there's an amusing conclusion to the story. One of my favorite versions is the fellow who wished for a thousand more wishes!

But what if that story really happened? Not with the genie in a bottle, but with the Lord telling someone, as He once told Solomon, "Ask whatever you wish of Me."

Something funny or smart alecky doesn't seem to fit, does it? Now we have a situation where the Sovereign Lord has posed the possibility. He deserves serious thought and a careful reply.

We know Solomon's request for wisdom to govern Israel, and we know God's answer to the request.

What is even more exciting is the realization that Psalm 37:4 tells us that I too can have the desires of my heart. This is Scripture about the Eternal God, not some fairy tale about a genie in a bottle!

But there is a catch: He gives me the desires of my heart only when I delight myself in Him. Delighting myself in the Lord God changes me. It changes the things I desire. God doesn't desire great wealth, the way selfish humans do. He doesn't desire long life – why should He? He's eternal already! What does God really desire?

He desires fellowship with human beings. He wants the broken relationships caused by sin renewed. He wants His creation to be restored to the way it was created to function.

These things will come to pass, as surely as God is always in control. If we delight ourselves in Him, we desire these things and pray that His Kingdom will come and His will be done on earth as it is in heaven. This is how delighting ourselves in the Lord ultimately brings about the desires of our hearts.

When we want what He wants, we get what we want!

64. TREASURE IN A CLAY POT

"But we have this treasure in jars of clay to show that this all-surpassing power is from God and not from us" (II Corinthians 4:7).

One of the important lessons taught to Balaam when the Lord let his donkey see what he didn't see and opened his donkey's mouth to rebuke him for his rebelliousness to the Lord is that speaking God's Word is a privilege as much as it is a calling. If you and I won't speak what God wants us to say, He could open an animal's mouth to get the job done!

Consider this, though: Of all the messages in all of world history, nothing is greater than the Gospel of Jesus Christ! Despite the fact that the Lord has a host of heavenly messengers we call angels, we never read one instance of an angel delivering the Gospel. An angel appeared to Cornelius and told him to send to Joppa for a human being named Peter to tell him the words of life. It was Peter who preached the Gospel.

For that matter, the Lord Jesus Himself appeared to Saul of Tarsus on the Damascus road, but the only instruction Jesus gave Saul was to continue into the city. There, a man by the name of Ananias was sent by the Lord to preach the Gospel to him.

I cannot explain why the Lord would leave such an essential task to us human instruments, except that I believe He knows what He is doing. Paul describes the call of preaching the Gospel as being a clay jar with a valuable treasure hidden in it.

The reason? Well, if something so powerful as the Gospel comes through a human instrument, it is obviously a Divine Power behind it greater than the messenger ever could be!

What a privilege to contain the Gospel of Jesus Christ in our own lives!

65. TOO PRECIOUS TO DRINK

"David longed for water and said, 'Oh, that someone would get me a drink of water from the well near the gate of Bethlehem!' So the three mighty warriors broke through the Philistine lines, drew water from the well near the gate of Bethlehem and carried it back to David. But he refused to drink it; instead, he poured it out before the Lord" (II Samuel 23:15).

I first heard this account of the three warriors who broke through the enemy lines to get David a taste of the water he craved when I was a kid in Sunday School. It was a hard thing for a kid to fathom why he would take something he had so craved after it had finally been given him and pour it out on the ground. But David wasn't simply wasting this precious water; he was turning it into an offering to God. He "poured it out before the Lord."

The blood of Jesus poured out on the Cross is hard to fathom too. It is more precious than we deserve. It cost God His Only Begotten Son. His life was in His blood. He was the perfect, sinless man; while we are all fallen, sinful human beings. Yet God poured Him out for us all, His precious blood spilled on the ground!

Sometimes we decline a generous offer because it is undeserved. But what if it is desperately needed? What if the bottle given to us at great cost to someone else was the only antidote to a deadly condition we had? Would we pour it out? Would it be appropriate under those circumstances to refuse?

This is the blood of the Son of God which was poured out for us. It is not to be wasted!

66. SURELY NOT I?

"While they were reclining at the table eating, he said, 'Truly I tell you, one of you will betray me-one who is eating with me.'

"They were saddened, and one by one they said to him, 'Surely you don't mean me?'' (Mark 14:18, 19).

At the outbreak of the Black Sox Scandal in 1920 a memorable quote was stamped on the pages of sports history – a young boy saying to Shoeless Joe Jackson, "Say it ain't so!" There are some things we desperately wish aren't true.

There is a way in New Testament Greek, to pose a question where the questioner seeks a negative answer. Such was the case at the Last Supper, when Jesus revealed to the Twelve that one of them would betray Him. Every one of them was shocked at this news. It was unthinkable. But they knew the Lord understood what was coming down. In self-doubt, they responded to the revelation that one of them would betray Jesus with the question, "Surely you don't mean me?"

It was a question, not a statement. The human heart is desperately wicked, and it is shocking enough to realize that it was one of this select group who would betray Jesus. More upsetting was the self-doubt the revelation evoked. It could be me! Please, Lord, say it isn't me!

Judas asked the question too, and the Lord gave an insightful response: "If you say so."

It could be any one of us. We all have the potential to let the Lord down and turn against Him at a critical moment. But the Lord also advises us it doesn't have to be so. Sure, we can stumble as did Peter and deny Him when the chips are down, but even then He is willing to restore us and equip us to do great things for Him.

Our self-doubt can be a good thing, if it makes us more dependent upon Jesus for our strength. At the Lord's Table, it is a good thing to examine ourselves and realize our own limitations: "Surely you don't mean me?"

There are those who will let the Lord down, but it doesn't have to be me!

67. HELP MY UNBELIEF!

"'If you can'? said Jesus. 'Everything is possible for one who believes.'

"Immediately the boy's father exclaimed, 'I do believe; help me overcome my unbelief!'" (Mark 9:23, 24).

It was a desperate situation, and the man who stood before Jesus with his problem had some measure of faith. It's quite possible that he even had more faith than Jesus' disciples, because Jesus told them after the event they were unable to help the boy with the epileptic demon because of their lack of faith. In contrast, the man had come to them with his tormented son because he believed they could do something for him. Alas! For whatever reason, these disciples of Jesus who had cast out demons from others could not cast out the demon that gave his son epileptic seizures.

At just the right moment, Jesus reappeared from an extended absence up on the mountain with His inner circle. Maybe the disciples couldn't do anything, but there was still Jesus to ask!

A brief description of the problem and the inability of Jesus' followers to help caused Jesus to deal with the tormented boy. Even as the child was brought to Jesus, the demon started in again, casting the boy on the ground and jerking his muscles with uncontrollable spasms. The desperate father opened his soul with words that were more than simply a poor choice, they reflected the spiritual warfare he had tried to wage alone – a warfare he was losing. "If you can do anything, take pity on us and help us!"

With that, Jesus gave the rebuke we quoted in the opening text. "If I can"? "If I can"? "Everything is possible to the person who believes!"

His response reflects not just the father, but the disciples who couldn't drive out the demon. It reflects us too, if we are honest enough to admit it.

"Lord, I do believe; help me overcome my unbelief!"

Here is a moment of faith stretching, a time where we admit our limitations to ourselves when we confess them to the Lord. Even though, we can feel His gentle rebuke for our lack of faith, He doesn't turn us away. He shoulders our problems and helps our unbelief.

We come to Him desperate, doubting, helpless. He challenges the faith that betrays weakness in the words, "If you can." We confess. He rebukes our problems and restores our broken lives to us, whole again!

68. ONE THING I DO KNOW

"He replied, 'Whether he is a sinner or not, I don't know. One thing I do know. I was blind but now I see!'" (John 9:25).

It was a classic "David versus Goliath" situation – the scholarly leaders of Jerusalem cross-examining a man who, until just a few hours earlier, had been a blind beggar. Could he even read? The average Jewish man could read, but Braille hadn't been invented yet; and he hadn't seen anything earlier than when he had opened his eyes at the pool of Siloam. He was unlearned, a nobody. To make it worse, he had lived under the cloud that somebody had done something terrible for him to have been born blind. That made him a social outcast.

Yet here he was speaking to the scholars with a line of reasoning so powerful they finally cast him out of the Temple because they couldn't refute his logic. Just as the Gospel of Jesus Christ in a short while would shame the wise men of the world, this simple beggar would put down their claims by stating what he had experienced firsthand. That morning he had been a beggar, blind since birth. Now, he could see! Jesus had opened his blind eyes.

Evangelism isn't something learned in Bible college. It is learned in the crucible of our own lives. Our best, our most irrefutable evidence isn't what we read in a book or heard from preachers; it's what we have personally experienced.

Our eyes weren't all blind from birth as this man's eyes were, but our lives were twisted and ruined in other ways before Jesus came. If He has truly intersected our own lives and changed us, we have concrete evidence of His power. Once we were (Put your own former, sin-tainted description here), but now we (Show us how Christ has changed you here).

Evangelism is like testifying in court – no hearsay, no speculation, just what you yourself have experienced. You are the expert witness as to what Jesus has done in your life!

69. DO YOU KNOW WHO YOU'RE TALKING TO?

"Jesus answered her, 'If you knew the gift of God and who it is that asks you for a drink, you would have asked him and he would have given you living water.'" (John 4:10).

"Do you know who you're talking to?" The question is usually poised by a person caught up in his self-importance. It's a threat to make things miserable for the hapless individual who hears it.

I knew a preacher who was reading a book on "awareness" while he waited for his order in a coffee shop in Laguna Beach, California back in the early 1970's. He congratulated himself for putting the book into practice even as he read it. The man next to him at the counter was looking around for something, and the preacher asked, "Do you need something?"

"Yeah," replied the man. "Can you pass me the sugar?"

Dutifully, the preacher handed the man the sugar and congratulated himself on his newfound powers of awareness. This continued when the waitress brought him his order. The preacher noticed people around the coffee shop whispering in excited tones.

"What's happened?" he asked her.

"Why, you handed him the sugar! Didn't you see who that was?"

It was John Wayne!

The Samaritan woman at the well of Sychar had several things to wonder about, especially that a Jewish man would ask her for a drink of water. First, she was a Samaritan. Then, she was a woman. Men didn't talk with women in public places, and Jews had nothing to do with Samaritans! But Jesus threw another surprise her way.

She had no idea she was in the presence of Messiah. Jesus said if she had known she would have asked *Him* for living water.

Sometimes we forget the power of God and the presence of Christ. We say prayers for healing and traveling mercies, but how many ask for the Living Water? It isn't a threat; it's an invitation that causes Jesus to ask us: "Do you know Who you're talking to?"

Lord, open our eyes! Bring us to our senses!

70. NOBODY CAN DO THAT!

"Daniel replied, 'No wise man, enchanter, magician or diviner can explain to the king the mystery he has asked about, but there is a God in heaven who reveals mysteries. He has shown King Nebuchadnezzar what will happen in days to come" (Daniel 2:27, 28).

"They said it couldn't be done.
With a smile, he went right to it.
He tackled the thing that couldn't be done
And found that he couldn't do it!"

Sorry, I just had to get that little quote in sometime or another!

But you and I know there are some things that cannot be done. Science understands how to transform matter into energy. It's how we generate electricity and heat our houses. But no one knows how to transform energy back into matter, Gene Roddenberry's idea of a transporter in Star Trek notwithstanding.

We don't know how to get perpetual motion, how to make something truly eternal. There is no perfect conservation of energy, not as we know it.

Nebuchadnezzar had a startling dream. Maybe like so many dreams you and I have, he was unable to recall it. Maybe he just wanted to see just how wise his "wise men" really were! Whatever the reason, he demanded that his advisors either tell him what the dream was he had dreamed, or he would have them all summarily executed!

Daniel and his friends sought the Lord for the dream, and the Lord revealed it. But when Daniel was taken to Nebuchadnezzar who asked him if he could tell what his dream had been.

"Nobody can do that!"

Can't you imagine what went through Nebuchadnezzar's mind for just a moment – that moment after Daniel said, "Nobody can do that," and what he said next?

"But there is a God in heaven…." This turned it all around. Daniel had indeed seen the king's vision, and he knew what it meant!

Eternal life? Nobody can do that!

Forgiveness of sins so that tainted mankind can stand purified? Nobody can do that!

A new heaven and new earth where things don't run down and go wrong? Nobody can do that!

But there is a God in Heaven Who does all of this and more! This is the God we celebrate!

71. SOMEONE TO STAND IN THE GAP

"I looked for someone among them who would build up the wall and stand before me in the gap on behalf of the land so I would not have to destroy it, but I found no one" (Ezekiel 22:30).

Behavioral researchers have found that peer pressure can cause an individual to say something he knows isn't true. In a simple test of 12 trained actors in a room with one test subject, when the instructions were given and even repeated that they should raise their hands for the shorter of two lines, as long as the 12 actors raised their hands for the longer line, so did the test subject. But when just one of the actors would actually follow the directions and raise his/her hand for the shorter of the two lines the test subject would most likely also follow through on the instructions. One person doing what was right had that powerful an influence on another.

God's message through Ezekiel is depressing. The people of Judah continued in their sin and their laughable solutions to the coming judgment. God said He looked for just one man to plead on behalf of the people, one person who would rebuild a wall of righteousness which could withstand judgment, one person who would stand in the gap between what the people deserved and what God truly desired to give them – but there was nobody.

Moses once interceded for the people of Israel when God was ready to smite them all. Jonah once preached of coming judgment and turned the entire city of Nineveh around. It doesn't take a majority to make a difference, not even a large minority – just one person willing to build up the wall and stand in the gap.

When D.L. Moody was just starting in the ministry he heard a preacher say, "The world has yet to see what God can do with a man fully surrendered to Him." Moody that night said, "By God's grace I'll be that man!"

God, make me one who will stand in the gap!

72. THAT'S WHY THIS DISTRESS

"Surely we are being punished because of our brother. We saw how distressed he was when he pleaded with us for his life, but we would not listen; that's why this distress has come on us" (Genesis 42:21).

It had been at least 15 years since Joseph's brothers had done him wrong. When they last saw him, he was an older teenager, pleading for mercy while they sold him into slavery – sent him far away into parts unknown from which he would never return. Joseph had gone through the whole gamut of emotions, advancing only to get knocked down for doing what was right, being forgotten in prison by an ungrateful butler, then being elevated to Prime Minister of Egypt, second only to Pharaoh. Now, despite the fact that Joseph had all but been purged of the bitter memories of the past, here they were bowed in his presence just as he had dreamed over 15 years earlier.

Joseph was clean shaven and well dressed – just as anyone would expect of an Egyptian lord, while his brothers looked very much the same as they had when they sold Joseph to the Midianite traders. He recognized them; they didn't have a clue who accused them of spying. He spoke through an interpreter.

So we read the revelation that brought Joseph to tears. For so long Joseph had thought they had gotten away with doing him this evil, but when they spoke Hebrew among themselves they didn't realize the Egyptian lord understood every word they said. Everything they said was ironically true. Joseph *was* accusing them of spying because of what they had done to him long ago. God *had* orchestrated the famine to bring them there, bowing before him. But beyond that was the revelation to Joseph that they hadn't gotten away with what they had done at all!

Obviously, every time something had gone wrong in their lives over the past 15 years, they connected it with the sin their guilty hearts couldn't escape. "This is happening because of what we did to Joseph!" They weren't prosperous, evil geniuses; they were pathetic slaves to their own accusing hearts. It was enough to make an Egyptian lord leave the room to cry his eyes out!

Never underestimate the haunting nature of guilt! The smug citizens of this world who mock Christ hide tortured hearts that accuse them at every misfortune. If you bear it, seek out the chance to confess the wrong. If you have suffered the wrong, quit brooding about it, and let God work out the opportunity to tell the person you forgive!

73. A KING TO WHOM JOSEPH MEANT NOTHING

"Then a new king, to whom Joseph meant nothing, came to power in Egypt" (Exodus 1:8).

"Freedom is always just one generation from extinction!" quoted Ronald Reagan in a speech in 1961. The history of Israel in Egypt confirms that idea. They had moved to Egypt as honored guests. When a new king, to whom Joseph meant nothing came to power in Egypt, they were enslaved.

Joseph had preserved Egypt from starvation and turned the nation into the economic colossus of the ancient world. He had made Pharaoh the richest, most powerful man in the world! The best thing Pharaoh had ever done in his entire life was to put Joseph in charge of everything and stand out of his way.

As long as that king was alive, Joseph and his kinsmen were respected. It wasn't that way in this subsequent generation. Someone had failed to study history. Someone had failed to give thanks.

There is a reason the Lord told Israel through Moses to place reminders everywhere about the Law and the Covenant. Moses told the Israelites that almost as soon as they would settle in the Promised Land they would forget the Lord their God. It's not just freedom that faces extinction in the next generation. It's our walk with the Lord.

It behooves us to remember, to continue in the breaking of bread, to read in the Bible what God has done every day. If we forget, we fail to give thanks. If we fail to give thanks, we lose sight of just where it was we came from.

"Bless the Lord, oh my soul
And forget not all His benefits" – Psalm 103:2.

74. HE WILL RAISE US UP ON THE THIRD DAY

"Come, let us return to the Lord.
For He has torn, but he will heal us;
He has stricken; but He will bind us up.
After two days He will revive us;
On the third day He will raise us up,
That we may live in His sight" (Hosea 6:1, 2 [NKJV]).

What had been a simple figure of speech became a word of prophecy. Hosea had waxed poetic in the start of this passage. He was calling the wayward northern kingdom of Israel back to the Lord God. They had gone through way too many kings, been overrun with foreign powers repeatedly, and suffered the loss of crops and property to all kinds of plagues. When Hosea spoke of the Lord restoring the fortunes of Israel, he used a figure of speech, a common reference to something happening on the third day – after just a short wait.

From our perspective, though, it is far more than a figure of speech. Jesus was raised from the dead on the third day. More than the fortunes of Israel were restored on the third day.

And Hosea speaks of our being raised up on the third day. The celebration of the resurrection is a celebration of victory over sin for us. All that sin had robbed from us, all that death had claimed and held in prison, everything else that reflected the sin of Adam on the world and our own sins over our own lives – all of it ended in just a short while. After three days, it was all turned back.

75. THE WRONG STUFF

"You desire but do not have, so you kill. You covet but you cannot get what you want, so you quarrel and fight. You do not have because you do not ask God. When you ask, you do not receive, because you ask with wrong motives, that you may spend what you get on your pleasures" (James 4:2, 3).

What do you want to hear your doctor say? "Everything seems to be fine" or "You have a mass in your body that could be cancerous"?

Naturally, we'd all love to hear everything is fine, but would you really want the doctor to say everything is fine if there really was a mass that could be cancerous? More than anything, we want the truth.

Considering James wrote his letter to Christians, it's shocking to see some of the things he says are going on in their lives. In the two verses we just read, he spoke of lusting, killing, coveting, quarreling, fighting, neglecting to pray and (when they do pray) praying for the wrong things, things to satisfy their sensual desires.

Things don't go well for churches where carnality persists. To be friends with the world aligns us as enemies of God, because the world opposes God. If someone pushes against God, God will ultimately push back.

Sure, there are brighter, more positive things James could write about. In fact he does mention brighter things elsewhere in this letter. But when something is wrong, you have to address the problem. Otherwise, it will never be addressed, never go away.

The lives of Christians were full of the wrong stuff. It needed to get washed off with strong detergent and a thorough scrubbing.

76. THE EXTENDED SCEPTER

"The king was sitting on his royal throne in the hall, facing the entrance. When he saw Queen Esther standing in the court, he was pleased with her and held out to her the gold scepter that was in his hand. So Esther approached and touched the tip of the scepter" (Esther 5:2).

When you live in a completely different culture you might not be able to appreciate the meaning of some actions in a setting apart from your own.

We don't have a king with a throne room. We don't live in a male-dominated society with laws on the books meting out severe penalties for a wife refusing to do something insulting commanded by her husband. This was the society in which Esther found herself. Ahasuerus was a male chauvinist in the classic sense. As a king, his word was law. Whatever pleased him was given favorable status. Whatever displeased him was removed from his sight immediately, and most often, permanently!

It was in this context that Esther was compelled to appeal on behalf of her people. Even though the law had been given irrevocably; and the Jews were doomed, Esther had limited influence and authority. Other laws on the books made it a dangerous thing for the queen to "call her husband at the office." She could approach the throne room, but only at serious risk to her own life. If the king did not approve of her presence that day – off with her head!

After a period of prayer and fasting, Esther dressed herself to look as attractive to the king as was possible and dared to make the risky appearance. What we just read in the Scripture text is the dramatic highlight of the story, because there was no telling how the king might respond. Don't take for granted that he would extend the royal scepter, because this was the same king who had deposed the queen just before Esther. Furthermore, he hadn't even talked with Esther for the prior month!

In the same way, we too consider approaching the King of the Universe; and we can't take our acceptance for granted. He is holy and just. He is immortal, invisible, and dwells in unapproachable light. Lesser kings wouldn't give us the time of day if we asked them. Why should the King of Kings care about us?

But the scepter has been extended! For whatever reason He may have, the King is delighted we came to His throne! This is an honor we must never presume.

77. IS IT WELL?

"So it was, when the man of God saw her afar off, that he said to his servant Gehazi, 'Look, the Shunammite woman! Please run now to meet her, and say to her, "Is it well with you? Is it well with your husband? Is it well with the child?"'"

"And she answered, 'It is well.'" (II Kings 4:25, 26 [NKJV]).

"I'd give anything to do that!" I caught myself saying that when I listened to Raphael Mendez, the world's greatest trumpeter of his day, in concert. I was just a grade school kid, learning the elementary aspects of playing a trumpet in band. As Mendez introduced the next encore he was going to play (out of six encores that night), he prefaced it by saying he had practiced at it as a teenager. "And by 'practice,'" he said, "I mean eight hours a day."

My heart sank. I had only kidded myself when I said I would give anything to play the trumpet like that. What it really cost I was unwilling to give.

I think we read the roll call of the faithful in Hebrews 11 and whisper to ourselves that we would be willing to give whatever it takes to be included in that list too. The Shunammite woman is the one most likely referred to when we hear about those who "received their dead back to life." Her son, who had been given her for showing hospitality to Elisha, expressly as a gift from God, was now cruelly taken from her in just a few minutes of sickness. As the account unfolds, she doesn't bury the boy, she doesn't tell her husband. Instead, she saddles her donkey and heads out immediately to find Elisha. Her actions say she believes Elisha will raise her son back to life!

Her words say the same thing. The passage cited tells us that Elisha knew something was wrong for her to be coming to him. He inquired about her health, her husband's health, her son's health. Each time, he asked, "Is it well?" Each time, she responded, "It is well."

Are we willing to give such an answer when our world comes crashing in on us? Grief and tribulation are the necessary backdrop for pictures of faith and triumph. In spite of all that, is it still well with us?

It is another story of loss and grief that lies behind H.G. Spafford's poem "It is Well With My Soul." To retell it here would be too much. But the loss of his wealth and all of his children in just a few months made him to reflect on the faith of this Shunammite woman so that her words became his own – "It is well!" Spafford passed through the darkness and emerged into the brightness of God's grace on the other side of his grief.

Is it well with you?

78. FREE? YEAH, RIGHT!

"Come, all you who are thirsty, come to the waters;
and you who have no money, come, buy and eat!
Come, buy wine and milk without money and without cost
Why spend money on what is not bread,
and your labor on what does not satisfy?" (Isaiah 55:1, 2).

"Order now, and we'll throw in a second worthless gizmo absolutely free! Just pay a separate fee."

Am I the only person who gets cynical when I hear "free" offers like that? How much are the shipping and handling costs? What is the true value of the item offered to me twice? Does it do what it claims to do? How can the people pushing this product afford to run these ads and still give out these wonderful devices free?

There are things that really are free. They are few and far between, and invariably they are offered truly for free only because someone else has paid for them. Such is the case of the waters, wine, and milk offered in Isaiah 55. Our Benefactor is the Lord God, the Creator of all things. If He can call the universe into existence by the word of His mouth, God is certainly able to give us generous gifts without it breaking Him.

We can understand why some people are still cynical about the idea of grace. If the offer sounds too good to be true it usually *is* too good to be true. But here, the account of the Father sending His Only Begotten Son to pay our sin debt is confirmed in the fact that He raised Jesus from the dead to declare Him to be everything He claimed.

This is one offer that really is free! Examine it, and you'll find in the small print all the confirmation you didn't expect to find!

Don't waste effort and money on something far less – especially if it has a separate fee!

79. FROM "DUSTIFIED" TO JUSTIFIED

"For if, by the trespass of the one man, death reigned through that one man, how much more will those who receive God's abundant provision of grace and of the gift of righteousness reign in life through the one man, Jesus Christ!" (Romans 5:17).

When Adam sinned, a host of things happened. Thorns and thistles came up in the ground to make thwart their labors in the field. Their labors would be accomplished only after drudgery (the sweat of their brow). Finally, to all of their descendants, death would enter into. From dust Adam had been made; to dust his body would return.

Our physical nature is the just that – dust. When we die, our mortal bodies break down and return to a few simple elements of earth.

When Jesus died, a host of things were reversed. The corrupted world was given the promise of restoration to a new order where things will no longer run down. The physical law of entropy will be repealed. Our labors will be creative, enjoyable, no longer a drudgery. But most of all, we will become partakers in eternal life with resurrection bodies like that of Jesus – bodies which will never grow old and die.

In the First Adam, we were "dustified," condemned to have our bodies laid in the earth to return to the natural elements from which it had been so fearfully and wonderfully made. In the Second Adam, we are justified. In the one man's sin we all died. In the second one man's act of righteousness we are all brought into eternal life.

80. FOOLISHNESS GREATER THAN PHILOSPHY

"Where is the wise person? Where is the teacher of the law? Where is the philosopher of this age? Has not God made foolish the wisdom of the world? For since in the wisdom of the God the world through its wisdom did not know him, God was pleased through the foolishness of what was preached to save those who believe" (I Corinthians 1:20, 21).

There was nothing wrong with Paul's sermon to a group of philosophers in Athens. He introduced it with a compliment to his audience. He presented it with sound logic. He even quoted from one of their own philosophers. But when Paul got to the centerpiece of the Gospel, the Resurrection of Jesus from the dead, they began to scoff him off Mar's Hill. The church Paul was able to start in Athens didn't compare to the church in Corinth.

Despite all its problems, and Paul dealt with a host of them, the church in Corinth grew and outstripped the church in Athens. Paul seems to reflect on the contrast between the two cities as he opens his letter to the Corinthians. The Athenians were "too smart for the Gospel." As such, they missed out on eternal life. The very message they mocked was God's ultimate triumph over the problem of evil in the world.

Paul spoke of His message as "the foolishness of God." So the Athenian philosophers had regarded it. In their snobbish wisdom, they had missed out on their only hope for eternal life.

Do you know people who reject the word of God because they think they know better? Are there passages of Scripture you yourself have dismissed because you think you know better? If we use our minds to dismiss ourselves from God, we're not using them the way He designed!

81. BREAK A LEG!

"Let me hear joy and gladness;
let the bones you have crushed rejoice.
Hide your face from my sins
and blot out all my iniquity" (Psalm 51:7-9).

"Break a leg" we would say to one another before a dramatic performance. It may sound strange, but that oft-repeated wish comes from a tradition that it is bad luck to wish an actor good luck before a performance. Consequently, rather than casting an evil spell over everything, you wish the actor would "break a leg."

When David poured out his heart in repentance for the sin he had committed by coveting another man's wife, committing adultery, and then committing murder in a vain cover-up, he wrote this passage about letting the bones the Lord had broken to rejoice. Sure, it's just poetry, and nobody expected David to be speaking of broken bones he had experienced at the time.

Still, there is an insight I have heard from others about what a shepherd would do with a lamb that was prone to wander. In order to keep the lamb from wandering off again and again, a shepherd would break the forelegs of the animal and then carry it around while the bones mended. By the time his legs had healed, the lamb would be so dependent upon the shepherd he was cured from wandering.

As a shepherd, David understood that "breaking a leg" was sometimes the best thing that could happen to a lamb. While his own bones weren't broken, he had suffered the loss of the child conceived by Bathsheba. He also had pronounced a judgment that would unfold as he lived out the rest of his life. Uriah was one man. David would pay fourfold by the deaths first of the baby, then of Amnon, then of Absalom, and (after David died) finally Adonijah. All that Nathan prophesied about sin and disgrace in the presence of all Israel happened during the rebellion of Absalom.

But the Lord also put away David's sin, so he would not die for it. David again wrote other psalms and found himself close to the Lord he had forsaken for awhile.

Broken bones aren't the worst thing that could happen to us!

82. NO MATTER WHAT

"King Nebuchadnezzar, we do not need to defend ourselves before you in this matter. If we are thrown into the blazing furnace, the God we serve is able to deliver us from it, and he will deliver us from Your Majesty's hand. But even if he does not, we want you to know, Your Majesty, that we will not serve your gods or worship the image of gold you have set up" (Daniel 3:16-18).

Let's face it: At one point or another, and more likely much more frequently than that, we have bargained with God. Abraham bargained with Him to spare his nephew Lot from the destruction of Sodom. Jacob bargained with God the morning he woke up from his vision of the golden staircase into heaven. Gideon asked for signs from the Lord.

That's what makes Shadrach, Meshach, and Abednego's reply to King Nebuchadnezzar so remarkable. No one could say they didn't know the consequences of refusing to bow to the king's image. The king himself had spelled them out and even taunted them with the claim that no god could deliver them from their fiery fate. They were apparently given an opportunity to talk it over among themselves so they could "come to their senses" and do what was reasonable – reasonable enough that everybody else had already done it.

But their reply was bold and memorable. No need to huddle. Contrary to what Nebuchadnezzar had said, their God *was* able to deliver them from the flaming furnace. They hadn't bargained with God about this, but even if He didn't save them they weren't going to compromise their determination to serve the Living God.

There have been times when the Lord God didn't intervene to rescue the ones determined to serve Him. Many Old Testament prophets were killed or imprisoned by tyrannical kings. Stephen was stoned to death. James the brother of John was put to death with the sword, and eleven other Apostles followed him in martyrdom during the formative years of the church. God doesn't owe us a long life on this corrupted, sin tainted world. For that matter, He doesn't owe us eternal life either; but He freely promises it through Jesus Christ.

True discipleship doesn't require time to "think it over" when the crisis comes. We should think these things over beforehand and be ready for the moment when we are brought before the tyrants of this world to test our faith. Those who trust God implicitly may not understand just how it is He will bring them through the trials facing them – only that He will.

83. TO GLORIFY GOD

"Jesus said this to indicate the kind of death by which Peter would glorify God. Then he said to him, 'Follow me'." (John 21:19).

If a person receives a love letter, he knows how to "read between the lines" of what his beloved has written to glean even more of a message. The same thing is true for a lawyer examining a contract from which he wants to weasel his way out! Obviously,
The inspired writers of Scripture have a way of clarifying things in their words and phrases so that even the incidental things command our attention. When we read them as a lawyer reads a contract, we become legalists who seek to find out just how much we can get away with. When we read them as love letter from God, we enrich ourselves with the most incidental of phrases.

When Jesus prophesied about how Peter would die in John 21, the usual route of thinking takes our minds to what traditional history tells us about Peter being crucified upside down. Not until we read the passage looking at the incidental language does it strike us that Peter would "glorify God" in the manner of death he died. Apparently, this phrase was commonly used in John's time in reference to how Christians died.

For the most part, we are like Peter before Jesus made this revelation to him. We don't know how we are going to die. Sure, if the doctor has told you that you're terminally ill, you have a fairly good idea; but most of us don't know if it will be sudden or lingering, as early as today or years later in the future.

John's terminology brings it all into focus. For the Christian, it isn't about the manner of death or the time of death; it's that we glorify God in our death. It is our final testimony to the lost world around us, to our brothers and sisters in Christ, to our family and loved ones. There should be a conscious determination in our hearts to glorify God when we die.

Several people become incapacitated before the time of transition. As long as the hospital requires a "living will" we should make certain that our objective in dying is "to glorify God." If others end up caring for us in our final days on this earth, they need to know we want to glorify God.

The world is dying to hear the Gospel. Let us make certain they hear the Gospel when we die!

84. COME AND SEE

"Philip found Nathanael and told him, 'We have found the one Moses wrote about in the Law, and about whom the prophets also wrote – Jesus of Nazareth, the son of Joseph.'

"'Nazareth! Can anything good come from there?' Nathanael asked.

"'Come and see,' said Philip" (John 1:45, 46).

Every classroom has the "brain." Every class has a cut-up. And every class has a "plodder." Jesus' class of twelve disciples was no exception.

Philip was Jesus' "plodder." He's the one who on the night before final exams (when Jesus was arrested) said, "Lord, show us the Father, and that will be sufficient." Three years of following Jesus, and Philip still didn't "get it."

Here, at the start of Jesus' ministry, Philip demonstrates his slowness. He tries to persuade Nathanael to follow Jesus of Nazareth, and Nathanael responds with cynicism: "Nazareth, eh? What good could ever come from there?"

Philip has never been eloquent. The only invitation he can offer is as plain as vanilla ice cream – artificially flavored vanilla ice cream at that!

"Come and see."

I heard of a small town church preparing for a crusade by sending out evangelistic teams two by two. An odd number showed up, leaving one person to go alone; and he was the oddest one of the number. The evangelism chairman realized that the mentally challenged man was limited, so he took the name of a local attorney who hadn't been to church in years – a member in name only and unlikely to come no matter who visited with him. This was the "prospect" this mildly retarded man was assigned to visit.

"Henry? What are you doing here?" the surprised attorney asked of the man who was too dull to understand he needed an appointment or that he should wait for the receptionist to let him back into the office.

"I come to talk to you about Jesus!" Henry couldn't say much, so he just blurted it out.

The lawyer started to hedge, "Well, Henry, I'm a very busy man; and I can't take good office time to…."

"Alright! Then go to hell!" Henry left as abruptly as he had entered.

The attorney called the preacher that night, admitting his

conscience was too troubled to let him sleep. He became an active member, a leader in the church, all because the dullest tool in the shed had been used by the Master Craftsman.

Philip's evangelism may have lacked eloquence. So did Henry's. But in both cases, it got the job done. Evangelism isn't eloquence. It's one beggar telling another beggar where to get a handout.

Don't wait for a college degree. Don't excuse yourself like Moses once tried, saying you don't have the necessary "way with words." Philip may not have been Jesus' brightest pupil, but Jesus knew why He called him.

85. THAT IN YOUR HAND

"Moses answered, 'What if they do not believe me or listen to me and say, "The Lord did not appear to you"?'

"Then the Lord said to him, 'What is that in your hand?'

"'A staff,' he replied." (Exodus 4:1, 2).

Improvisation is wonderful to observe. Jackie Chan fight sequences not only include his martial arts skills, but also improvisational use of things around him – a barrel, a ladder, a banner. I guess that's why his action movies are also considered a type of comedy.

MacGyver is on television – again! Why? It's hard to get away from our attraction to someone who can use whatever is available to accomplish what needs to be done.

There in front of the Burning Bush, Moses was offering his litany of excuses to the Lord, explaining why he wasn't the man to go to Pharaoh's court (where he had been raised for 40 years), to demand that Pharaoh release God's people (with whom Moses had chosen to identify himself), so they could come into the wilderness (where Moses had been herding sheep for his most recent 40 years).

His concern that the people wouldn't believe the Lord had sent him was responded to with a "MacGyver" from the Lord: "What's that in your hand?"

Every shepherd carried one of those things – a staff. It's okay when you're shepherding, but what does it have to do with becoming a fearless leader of a nation about to rebel against the most powerful nation in the world? Take the Lord God out of the equation, and Jackie Chan isn't going to be able to hold off the entire Egyptian army. Not even MacGyver could improvise with something so simple.

But don't take the Lord God out of the equation! The sign of throwing the rod on the ground and having it become a snake was impressive, but just a starter. Wait until Moses holds it over the Red Sea or uses it to bring forth water from a rock in the desert!

A little boy once shared his humble lunch of five barley rolls and two smoked fish. We know how the Lord "improvised" with that one too. Don't ever underestimate the ability of the Lord to do great things through you. Just answer the question, "What's that in your hand?" and turn it over to Him.

86. IN GOD'S IMAGE

"Then God said. 'Let us make mankind in our image, in our likeness, so that they may rule over the fish in the sea and the birds in the sky, over the livestock and all the wild animals, and over all the creatures that move along the ground.'

"So God created mankind in his own image,
in the image of God he created them:
male and female he created them" (Genesis 1:26, 27).

When people ask why it is alright to hunt animals and wrong to kill humans, the correct answer is found in this passage. Couple it with Genesis 9:3, and you see plainly that God gave Noah and his descendants animal flesh as a part of their diet after the flood. In that same passage, however, you will find that the Lord just three verses later says the shedding of human blood is forbidden, because man is made in God's image.

Animals have physical life. Humans have physical and spirit life, because God is a spirit being. Animals follow their own biological instincts. Humans have laws to keep. Animals are subject to human domination. Humans manage the animal population and are accountable when species are endangered.

The irony of the temptation of Eve in the Garden of Eden was the lie Satan told her about the forbidden fruit: "The day you eat the fruit you will become as God." Evidently Eve had forgotten for the moment – She already was as God! God had created her in His likeness. The moment she ate the fruit she drastically reduced her "godlikeness" by dying spiritually. Adam and Eve, the managers of all creation, became "dumb beasts" in their ambition to become as God!

Aesop once told the fable of a dog, bringing his bone home across a bridge. He looked over the edge of the bridge and saw his reflection in the water. Thinking it was another dog with a bigger bone he barked and dropped his bone into the water below. This has also become the plight of ambitious, rebellious mankind. We lost our godlikeness when we aspired to become as God.

It requires a New Creation through Jesus Christ to get God's image back and to empower us to live as the image-bearing creation we were intended to be.

87. LOVE BEFORE "FIRST SIGHT"

"Boaz replied, 'I've been told all about what you have done for your mother-in-law since the death of your husband – how you left your father and mother and your homeland and came to live with a people you did not know before. May the Lord repay you for what you have done. May you be richly rewarded by the Lord, the God of Israel, under whose wings you have come to take refuge.'" (Ruth 2:11, 12).

The story of Ruth is considered by many Bible teachers one of the greatest love stories in the Bible. I certainly am not about to contradict such a multitude of people who so assess it. But this is a love story that was made from much more than a couple of people who smiled at each other, decided the liked each other, fell in love, got married, and lived happily ever after!

Please note that Boaz admired Ruth before he ever laid eyes on her. By his own admission, he had heard talk around Bethlehem of the young Moabite widow who had accompanied her widowed mother-in-law back to Naomi's homeland. It meant leaving all her birth family, homeland, and home customs to come glean in the fields of Bethlehem to eek out a pauper's existence for the two of them. Though a newcomer in Israel, Ruth had already secured a good reputation among the people of Bethlehem. Boaz had heard the reports and was already inclined to look favorably upon the young woman. We don't dismiss the idea that she was also probably a good looking woman, but there was a beauty already present in her that Boaz perceived before he ever saw Ruth. This was even more compelling than "love at first sight"!

Such is the benefit of a good report for our lives. This is why Christians are repeatedly admonished to live out holy and godly lives in the communities where they dwell, to live (insofar as is possible for them) at peace with all men. They gain the treasure of good report among others, and it takes them far.

Look just how far a good report brought Ruth. She is in the genealogy of Jesus, our Savior!

88. THE GLORY OF CONFESSING SIN

"Then Joshua said to Achan, 'My son, give glory to the Lord, the God of Israel, and honor him. Tell me what you have done; do not hide it from me.'" (Joshua 7:19).

The only battle casualties recorded in the entire account of the conquest of Canaan, the book of Joshua, are 37. They all occurred with a smaller force which had been sent to deal with the smaller city of Ai after the conquest of the large city of Jericho. When Israel's troops had been driven back and the report of 37 losses was given to Joshua, he fell before the Lord and asked how the Lord could have failed His people.

As the story unfolded, Joshua found it wasn't the Lord who had failed. It was someone in Israel who had deliberately disobeyed the command-ments given about the spoils of Jericho. An assembly was called. Lots were drawn. Achan was singled out.

Joshua's command should clarify how God benefits when we confess our sins. Things go wrong for God's people when they sin. When God's people confess their sins it clarifies why they went wrong. Otherwise, it simply looks the way it did to Joshua after Israel's humiliation at Ai; it looked like God failed!

Of course, people of faith understand God doesn't fail. Unbelieving onlookers don't see it that way. This is why the Bible speaks of the enemies of God having opportunity to speak evil of Him when we do wrong. God has to stop blessing the people he wants to bless so He can take time out to discipline them!

Dale Carnegie's *How to Win Friends and Influence People* gives a similar piece of advice in this list of rules for getting people to like you: "When you are wrong, admit it quickly and emphatically!" For Christians, this is doubly true, since it takes the blame for what went wrong away from the God we serve.

89. DON'T QUARREL ALONG THE WAY

""""Then he [Joseph] sent his brothers away, and as they were leaving he said to them, 'Don't quarrel along the way!'"" (Genesis 45:24).

The first time Joseph had to leave the room to cry and then regain his composure after his brothers had bowed before him in Egypt was when he had heard them arguing among themselves about the wrong that had done to him over fifteen years earlier. Probably, Joseph had been under the misapprehension that they had completely gotten away with the wrong they had done to him. There had been no consequences they had suffered when they were paid money to sell their brother into slavery; Joseph had been the one who became a slave, an unjustly accused prisoner, a forgotten man wasting away in a prison in a foreign land.

Ah, but there *had* been consequences! Joseph understood every word they spoke among themselves in their Hebrew, and their conversation revealed that they had connected everything that had gone wrong in their lives with what they had done to Joseph all those years before. It was Moe, Larry, and Curly poking and slapping one another every time a new problem confronted them. Their guilt never left their minds for over fifteen years.

We tend to quarrel when things go bad. It is a dynamic I have observed in sports, in business, in politics, even in family life and church. Joseph knew his brothers were going to get back to their father and have to reveal how they had unnecessarily brought him to years of grieving by their deceit. This was not going to be easy! Wisely, he cautioned them against quarreling. Quarreling means we've "lost it" as far as our own plans and schemes are concerned. We are no longer in control.

But God had been in control! In the midst of the things they had actually meant for evil, God was at work to provide for all of them. Quarreling was just another expression of worry, and worry is the opposite of faith in God.

Don't worry! Don't quarrel! Have faith in God instead.

90. WHERE ARE YOU?

"Then the man and his wife heard the sound of the Lord God as he was walking in the garden in the cool of the day, and they hid from the Lord God among the trees of the garden. But the Lord God called to the man, 'Where are you?'" (Genesis 3:8, 9).

Can you imagine the childish foolishness, the utter futility, of Adam and Eve hiding from the Lord God when they heard Him walking in the garden in the cool of the day? God knows everything before it even happens! How couldn't He know exactly where Adam and Eve had been and what they had been up to? Either Adam and Eve were better at hiding than you and I will ever be, or God had something else in mind when He asked, "Where are you?"

Since there was nothing to be revealed to the God Who knows all things, the only thing to be revealed by His "Where are you?" question was what He wanted to reveal to these novice sinners.

They were alienated from God. Apparently, God walked with them in the Garden of Eden on a regular basis. This was the first time they hid when they heard God coming. Sin has an obvious way of separating us from our fellowship with God.

They were ashamed. It is a burning, helpless feeling that comes over us when we know we have done something wrong. We don't want it to be seen. We try all our "fig leaf" applications to the problem we created, and none of them work.

They were foolish. Just imagine Adam hiding behind a tree and saying, "Oh, please, wherever He looks, don't let Him look behind this tree!" Just as quickly it also hits him: "To whom am I praying?"

Just about any prayer that goes up from our lips makes us look rather puny, simply because it goes up from us to the Lord God, the omnipotent, omniscient, omnipresent Creator of all things. His question isn't because He can't see us where we are. It's because we need to see ourselves for where we are and what we've done!

When He calls to us, "Where are you?" may we look carefully upon our own plight and answer!

91. THE MEN WHO GAVE UP EVERYTHING

"The kingdom of heaven is like treasure hidden in a field. When a man found it, he hid it again, and then in his joy went and sold all he had and bought that field.

"Again, the kingdom of heaven is like a merchant looking for fine pearls. When he found one of great value, he went away and sold everything he had and bought it" (Matthew 13:44-46).

Dad's dumb jokes – oh, yes, I have my repertoire! I really like to tell them in front of the daughter who is most annoyed by them!

Get on a crowded elevator, turn around to face everybody else and say, "I suppose you're wondering why I called this meeting!"

Wait till the nurse brings out the blood pressure cuff at the doctor's office and say, "Do you know why they call that thing a blood pressure cuff? 'Cause that's easier to say than 'sphygmomanometer'!" It took a lot of practice pronouncing that word so I could tell that joke!

Here's an equally dumb riddle: Do you know why this couplet of parables isn't called "The Men Who Gave up Everything"?

It almost sounds like another really bad "Dad joke." These are separate parables, one called "The Hidden Treasure," the other "The Precious Pearl."

But they are told together, and it would be quicker to name the pair "The Men Who Gave up Everything," wouldn't it?

Maybe it would be a quicker title, but it doesn't really fit. The focus of these parables is not on what they gave up. True, both men gave up everything, but the real emphasis wasn't upon that. It was upon the hidden treasure and the precious pearl. It was on what they gained, not what they gave up!

It is equally "dumb" for us to look back on the things we gave up to follow Christ. It's like the former slaves in the wilderness who longed for "the good old days back in Egypt" – completely the wrong focus! All the other pearls in the merchant's collection combined couldn't equal the value of that one pearl of great price. All the possessions held by the man who found the hidden treasure weren't even worth describing in contrast to that hidden treasure.

Let's make sure the focus of our Kingdom walk is where it ought to be – not on what we gave up, but on what we gained!

92. AN ANTI-ANXIETY PRESCRIPTION

"Do not be anxious about anything, but in every situation, by prayer and petition, with thanksgiving, present your requests to God. And the peace of God, which transcends all understanding, will guard your hearts and your minds in Christ Jesus" (Philippians 4:6, 7).

They say eighty-five percent of the things people worry about never come to pass. A friend of mine heard this statistic and started to worry more often, thinking he was reducing the likelihood of the things he worried about coming pass by eighty-five percent! I expect, though, you have worried about things beyond your control the same way I have, from time to time.

Doctors prescribe "anti-anxiety" medications. As I hear the cautionary statements about possible side-effects for these meds I cringe: "May cause suicidal thoughts." That sounds an awful lot like something else to worry about! Is there something more effective for anxiety than meds, something with fewer dangerous side-effects?

The Apostle Paul follows his statement about not being anxious with alternative actions. Let's check out his regimen.

"In every situation…" applies his prescription to a daily basis. When times are good, and we are afraid to lose them; when times are bad, and we are afraid they will never stop; major times, minor times; long times, short times – in every situation we face, his solution to anxiety is appropriate.

"By prayer and petition…" covers several aspects of prayer beyond our prayer request lists. How about just acknowledging how great God is? How about remembering some of the great things God has done in history? How about confessing sins? We almost always have a "shopping list" when we enter into prayer, so the petitions we intend to bring will get said. And God doesn't mind our asking. After all, He knows how dependent we are upon Him.

"With thanksgiving…" reminds us to thank the Lord for prayers already answered and for prayers He is about to answer. He didn't have to let us into the Throne Room, seeing how He is the most powerful Ruler in the whole universe. It's quite a privilege to have His ear for whatever it was that brought us there.

The result? Peace! It is the peace of God that transcends all human understanding. It will guard our hearts and minds in Christ Jesus from every fear, every uncertainty that could loom before us.

Most of our anxiety can be diagnosed as a simple lack of faith in God. The more time we spend with Him, the easier it is to trust Him.

93. AN OVERWHELMING FORCE

"Do not be overcome by evil, but overcome evil with good"
(Romans 12:21).

J.R.R. Tolkien's trilogy *The Lord of the Rings* begins the three volume series with a problem of evil and a strategy to deal with it worth noting. The Dark Lord Sauron was searching for the ring of power, which had come into the possession of a Hobbit named Baggins. As a meeting between the good inhabitants of middle earth is held to determine what to do about the approaching storm in their world, it is decided the only way to thwart Sauron and his lust for the ring of power is to take the ring back to the flames of the volcanic Mt. Doom and throw it into the lava to destroy it in the same heat that had once forged it. The person appointed as the bearer of the ring was not a warrior, not one of the mighty elves, or a tough dwarf – rather the Hobbit Frodo Baggins.

This epic parallels in many ways the account we read in Scripture, as we see the secret plan of the Lord unfold on the pages of human history. Man had sinned and subjected all of mankind to death and all of the world to futility. The Lord's plan to redeem mankind and the fallen creation from the evil lord that had taken it prisoner was to send a Messiah not by means of a white charger, leading legions of angel warriors, but born as an ordinary baby, leading twelve men from common occupations, and making his Triumphal Entry on the back of a donkey colt. He would gain His eternal throne not with force, but by submitting Himself to an undeserved criminal's death on a cross.

Consider then how His followers are to overcome the forces of evil in their time here on earth: not as warriors, not even as skilled debaters. Our means of overcoming our enemies is by repaying the world's evil with good. Despite repeated Roman persecutions, despite being labeled as atheists, outlaws and outcasts, the early Church conquered the world that hated them.

It is a pattern to remember today when we consider the opposition to the church in our world. The only power great enough to overwhelm evil like a great tsunami is good. Wars may hold nations in check by force, but unfeigned goodness holds hearts forever.

94. BEHOLD, I THOUGHT…

"But Naaman was angry and went away, saying, 'Behold, I thought that he would surely come out to me and stand and call upon the name of the Lord his God, and wave his hand over the place and cure the leper.'" (II Kings 5:11).

The one-liners given about men are merciless, even if many of them are deserved! Men don't stop and ask for instructions. Men don't read the directions. Men don't listen to their wives when their wives are talking. On the list goes.

Just for the record, not all men are that way; and not all women are much better at asking for directions or listening when they are given. Still, it's appropriate to note how failing to follow instructions usually gets whoever fails to follow into even more trouble.

Naaman was a Syrian, not an Israelite. Desperate to be cured of his incurable skin disease, he went to Israel to have Elisha cleanse him in the name of the God of Israel. Being a high ranking officer gave Naaman an ego that got in the way of accepting how he was to be cured.

First, he was not greeted by Elisha himself. This was hardly the proper way to treat someone so high ranking and powerful as he. Naaman felt insulted by having a servant come to him with the instructions.

Then, there was the manner in which he was to be cleansed. He had expected some fanfare that would make more of a show of the whole event of his cleansing. Elisha should wave his hands toward heaven and chant whatever magical incantations prophets of the God of Israel would mutter. Instead, he was told to take a bath – dipping himself under the waters of the Jordan River seven times.

Even the river for his cleansing was an insult! Damascus had clean water in the Abana and Pharpar Rivers, and they were right in Naaman's home! The Jordan was muddy and not really much to look at.

But all the time Naaman ranted about how he thought it should've happened he was still a leper. In fact, he would never have been cured of leprosy if he hadn't listened to the humble pleas of his servants. When he finally did follow the instructions God had given him and dipped himself seven times in the Jordan, Naaman was cured.

There are still people today who refuse to follow God's instructions. They think it would be much more impressive if they did a long list of wonderful things to be saved. They balk at the simple washing in baptism that the Lord asked to be done to them. They think they know better than God what He can let slide and what He has to hold them accountable for.

Simply put: Learn from Naaman! If you want God to cleanse you, follow God's instructions!

95. TAKING STOCK IN THE RESERVES

"The Lord said to him [Elijah], 'Go back the way you came, and go
to the Desert of Damascus. When you get there, anoint Hazael king
over Aram. Also anoint Jehu son of Nimshi king over Israel, and
anoint Elisha son of Shaphat from Abel Meholah to succeed you as
prophet.... Yet I reserve seven thousand in all Israel – all whose
knees have not bowed down to Baal and whose mouths have not
kissed him.'" (I Kings 19:15-16, 18).

Elijah had just come down from his "mountain top experience"
on Mt. Carmel. It was probably the epitome of his career as a
prophet. Fire came down from heaven and not only consumed the
sacrifice on the altar he had built to the Lord, but also the stones
and the water in the ditch all around it. The pagan prophets who
had failed at getting Baal to send down fire on their altar were all
put to death by the zealous multitude. Everybody who saw the fire
from heaven was shouting that the Lord was the One True God.
The Lord God sent an abundance of rain that ended the three and a
half years' drought.

But Queen Jezebel had not attended the revival meeting on Mt.
Carmel. She pledged to have Elijah put to death. Elijah hightailed it
to the wilderness and was sent on to Mt. Horeb to await further
instruction from the Lord.

When the Lord appeared to Elijah, Elijah confessed to serious
depression. It didn't matter that he had defeated the prophets of
Baal. All that happened on Mt. Carmel was quickly forgotten by
the fickle crowds. Once again, he felt all alone in standing for the
Lord and righteousness. What's more, he was getting old. Elijah
wasn't sure he had any more "Mt. Carmels" left in him. What
would happen after he was gone?

The Lord addressed Elijah's concerns with multiple
instructions. The pagan Syrian king Hazael was to be anointed as
God's instrument of judgment on Israel. The military commander
Jehu was to be anointed as king over a new dynasty in Israel. And
Elijah was to mentor Elisha the son of Shapat as his successor.

The world would continue to turn without Elijah. He was a
great prophet, an important figure in the history of Israel. Yet
among human beings, no one is indispensable. We all say our lines
and act our parts on the stage of life, but as surely as we entered the
stage, we too shall exit.

The Lord's real "kicker" to Elijah's doldrums was the last thing He revealed. Elijah was far from alone! The Lord knew of 7,000 in Israel who hadn't compromised to worship Baal. Some of them were surely inspired by the courage of Elijah. His life may not have seemed that effective from where Elijah watched, but the Lord knew of a multitude.

Look around you, especially in the assemblies on the First Day! You're not alone! There are people you can look up to, and there are surely people who look up to you! There are even more than you can see who love the Lord with every ounce of their being. They break the bread with you.

96. WHO MAKES YOU SO DIFFERENT?

"For who makes you different from anyone else? What do you have that you did not receive? And if you did receive it, why do you boast as though you did not?" (I Corinthians 4:7).

As Paul chastised the Corinthians for being so puffed up about who had baptized them and what showy spiritual gifts they might have, he asked three questions that lay bare just how awful a sin it is to be ungrateful.

"Who makes you different from anyone else?" Do we not all have a birthday, a day when we will die, and a life in between? We have common needs, common concerns, common challenges. As my brother mimicked Mr. Rogers, "Remember, boys and girls, you're unique – just like everybody else!"

"What do you have that you did not receive?" There is no such thing as "a self-made man" unless it is the bum in the gutter. That's the only person who can really say he got himself to where he is today. If we have natural ability, it is the result of genetics from our parents. If we have an ability we learned, we have teachers and coaches who mentored us. If we succeeded at work, we were hired by someone in HR on behalf of the company. If we run our own business, we owe our success, in part at least, to the customers who sought our products or services. If you have no one to thank, you are the bum in the gutter, or worse, you are a pathetic ingrate!

"If you did receive it, why do you boast as though you did not?" The Corinthian Christians were Christians because they had received the Gospel from somebody else. They came from a multitude of backgrounds and had several Apostles or teachers to whom they owed their spiritual lives. This was an occasion for thanksgiving, not for boasting. We have eternal life because of what Christ did, most of all. After that, we have family and teachers who patiently taught us the Word of God and waited for us to make the Lord our Lord. Beyond that, we have Christian friends, preachers, church leaders, authors, and a host of others carrying us along in our walk with Jesus.

We're unique, just like everybody else!

97. THE EQUALIZER

"Believers in humble circumstances ought to take pride in their high position. But the rich should take pride in their humiliation – since they will pass away like a wild flower. For the sun rises with scorching heat and withers the plant; its blossom fall and its beauty is destroyed. In the same way, the rich will fade away even while they go about their business" (James 1:9-11).

There was a television series entitled "The Equalizer" with the premise that the main character (a CIA retiree) would help people who couldn't get help from law enforcement or the usual public agencies. He was the champion of the little guy, and everybody cheered to see the nobodies getting what they needed for justice against the ones who did them dirty.

James speaks of an equalizer which is not some fictional character portrayed by Edward Woodard on television. It is death. Yes, the poor are poor for now; but God will exalt the righteous for eternity when we all stand before His judgment throne. Furthermore, the moment the rich die, they become equal to the poor. Both are buried six feet under. Both stop breathing. Both take the same amount of wealth with them beyond the grave – nothing!

We aren't all equal now. We were created equally important in the Lord's eyes, but that quickly gets added to or subtracted from in the eyes of the world. Some have received more opportunity than others. Some have made a better accounting with what was given to them than others. Some have oppressed the poor and taken advantage of what little they have. Others have generously given to the poor, understanding the main reason the Lord enriched their lives was so they could be a blessing to others. There are a whole lot of different scenarios at play in the world around us, and the word "equality" doesn't come to mind as we observe them!

The time we spend together in the presence of the Lord gets us back to equality. He values the person to your right, the person to your left, the persons ahead you and behind you every bit as much as He values you. Yes, you are immeasurably important!

So are they!

98. THE NORTH STAR

"Jesus Christ is the same yesterday and today and forever" (Hebrews 12:8).

When wagon trains pushed westward in the 1800's there were no interstates or electronic GPS devices to help them navigate. Skilled wagon masters knew how to begin the day by locating a recognizable landmark along their path and aiming for the position they wanted relative to where the landmark stood. But as they crossed the open plains of Nebraska and Wyoming, sometimes familiar landmarks weren't to be seen on the horizon! That's why every night the sky was clear, the wagon master would find the North Star in the sky and point the wagon tongue on his supply wagon due north. The next morning, using a simple square or protractor, he could sight down the horizon due west and determine what lesser known landmark would be his objective for that day. The land was open enough that the 10-12 miles per day a wagon train averaged wouldn't take them beyond his farthest sighted landmark.

As the book of Hebrews winds down, the author reminds persecuted Jewish Christians that Jesus Christ is the Constant in their lives. He is the same, yesterday, today, and forever. He doesn't change.

The older we get, the more intimidating change becomes. No sooner do we listen to our music on one gadget than we find out all our recordings are obsolete and have to be transferred into a new format for a newer gadget. But the music genre has also changed, and our "oldies" are also obsolete! We adjust to the changes in government, and then elections upset the apple cart all over again! We master one routine at work, and then management announces – you guessed it – changes to improve things!

Jesus doesn't change. His word is constant. What He promised, He will do. What He has done cannot be undone. Perhaps best of all is the closing promise He made before He left: "I am with you always, even to the end of the world." Every night, we can go to sleep having taken our bearings from the North Star. Every morning, we can look over the coming day to find our goal and be sure it is exactly where we need to go.

99. DINING WITH A MISER

"⁶Do not eat the food of a begrudging host,
   do not crave his delicacies;
⁷for he is the kind of person
   who is always thinking about the cost.
"Eat and drink," he says to you,
   but his heart is not with you.
⁸You will vomit up the little you have eaten
   and will have wasted your compliments" (Proverbs 23:6-8).

Have you ever been given a gift with strings attached?

In a former ministry years ago, I had a fairly wealthy family that wanted to donate a new sound system to the church. It was appreciated since the old sound system had a technology that seemed to utilize smoke signals for transmission. However, as the new system was installed, and the equipment set up, it became apparent that this "gift" was going to be problematic.

The equalizer levels were set by the donor and not to be adjusted. The lavalier mic was to be used for the sermon and for the communion meditation. The speakers had to remain directed exactly as they had been set up, even if it meant feedback when the minister was down off the platform for invitation.

Briefly put, the new sound system wasn't as much a gift as it was a controlling interest in how several people conducted themselves during church!

The proverb we just read is about dining at the table of a stingy, rich man. He may have the finest of food on the table before you, and he certainly can afford it. But he also is unwilling to let go of what it cost him even as you eat it. Does this fine dining taste good to you? How could it? It may be called a free meal, but it isn't free at all!

Dining at the Lord's Table should be an enjoyable experience. Salvation is freely offered to all who come to God through Jesus Christ! Only if we perceive God as a terrible Judge Who will smack us down the moment we get out of line would we feel like we were dining with a miser. If so, then we have taken the joy out ourselves; because God chose to relate to us through the Son as His precious children. Children may not be entirely refined in their table etiquette, but they know how to enjoy food offered at a table where they are loved!

100. REMEMBER ME FOR GOOD

"Remember me, O my God, for good!" (Nehemiah 13:31b [NKJV]).

As a president nears the end of his time in office, the media focuses upon what they call his "legacy." This, in a nutshell, is what people are most likely to remember about the time he was in office. With Lincoln, it was the Civil War. With Franklin Roosevelt, it was the Great Depression and WW II. With Nixon, it was Watergate. With Clinton, it was Lewinsky.

Not that these presidents didn't accomplish many, many other things while in office. It's just that our minds make abbreviated associations with each one, and those brief thoughts become their "legacies."

A history of the rebuilding of Jerusalem after the Captivity is recorded by the governor appointed to the task, Nehemiah. Of all the problems he faced down and waywardness by the returned remnant itself, Nehemiah makes his closing comment about his legacy in God's eyes. He could be remembered for the task of rebuilding the city wall in the face of fierce opposition. Indeed, this is how artists depict Nehemiah. He could be remembered for the reforms he initiated, ending usurious interest on loans of wealthy Jews to their kinsmen. He could even be remembered for his own "Watergate"! You see, the book of Law was publicly read for the first time to this generation at the Watergate of the city.

What did Nehemiah desire to be his legacy? He wanted the favor of the Lord. Nehemiah wanted God to smile whenever his name was mentioned in heaven.

I smile when I hear the name of my wife, my children, my grandchild-ren. I smile when I remember people with whom I have labored in the Lord. I smile at the mention of my parents and the large number of siblings I grew up with. These have all been the best moments of living on this planet.

We should smile at the Table of the Lord and remember Him with our sincerest of favor, an undying gratitude for the One Who dared to die for us.

Jesus smiled when He remembered us. Isaiah prophesied of Jesus' passion:

"He shall see the labor of His soul, and be satisfied.
By His knowledge My righteous Servant shall justify many,
For He shall bear their iniquities" (53:11 [NKJV]).

101. COME BEFORE WINTER!

"Do your utmost to come before winter." (II Timothy 4:21a [NKJV]).

Native Americans personified opportunity as a beautiful maiden who walked by very quickly. Her long hair hung down over her face, signify-ing that if you did not seize her as she came, you would have no means to grasp her after she had gone by. So it is with so many things in life. What was possible today is no longer offered if we put it off until tomorrow. We can spend eternity in regret for having not taken advantage in time, but we still will not find the chance again.

Paul was writing his final letter to Timothy. His execution would occur soon, and he wanted one last visit, face to face, with this young man he had chosen to train to carry on the work of the ministry of the Gospel of Jesus Christ. If Timothy tarried until winter came, there were a couple of reasons why it would be too late. The first reason was the capricious Emperor Nero. His hatred for Christians had ramped up the first major persecution by the Roman government. Paul's Roman citizenship notwithstanding, Nero was going to see the Christian leaders were "taken care of" in such a way that people would think twice about becoming a part of this outlaw religion

The second was the way seasons predictably work. Winter was impossible to travel by ship over the Mediterranean Sea. Remember Paul's shipwreck in Acts 27? That's what happens when travelers take off too late in the fall for a Mediterranean Sea cruise!

The tasks the Lord calls us to do are not to be procrastinated. Sometimes, those opposed to the Gospel will hamper the work enough we will never get it done if we delay. Then, the seasons of life inevitably slow us down or stop us altogether from finishing. We become disabled. Our bodies are weaker and slower, and our minds don't recall things as quickly as they once could. We need to make the most of every opportunity because the days are evil (Ephesians 5:16).

What if Timothy didn't make it before winter? What if he arrived at the Mamertine Prison in Rome the following spring only to find that Paul had been executed a week earlier? If you understand regret, you can also appreciate the urgency in Paul's request.

"Do your utmost to come before winter!"

102. WHERE CAN I GO FROM YOUR PRESENCE?

"^{7}Where can I go from your Spirit?

Where can I flee from your presence?

^{8}If I go up to the heavens, you are there;

if I make my bed in the depths, you are there.

^{9}If I rise on the wings of the dawn,

if I settle on the far side of the sea,

^{10}even there your hand will guide me,

your right hand will hold me fast" (Psalm 139:7-10).

In this Psalm, David marvels in the perfect wisdom of God. He knows us better than we know ourselves. He knows what we will say and do before we even decide to say and do it. He knows our thoughts, both good and evil.

In panic, David first considers trying to hide from the presence of God. Of course, it doesn't take long for anyone to realize just how futile that would be! Adam tried to hide in the bushes. Jonah tried to flee to Tarshish. Fat chance any of us would have trying to escape the seeing eyes of the Lord!

Then, in midsentence, David's panic turns to comfort. If he ascended to the heights of heaven or the depths of the cold, dark earth, even if he could fly away beyond the farthest reaches of the sea – God's right hand will guide him and hold him fast. The Omniscient, Omnipresent God wasn't that bad an arrangement when you think more deeply about Him!

We panic when we think of God knowing our innermost thoughts. Our thought lives are embarrassing! Despite the fact the Lord knows us that well, we soon realize He still loves us. We may have squandered our inheritance from Him on riotous living in the far country, but His heart has followed us every wayward step there. He longs for the day we come trudging home. It's no longer as embarrassing to us when we understand His acceptance and forgiveness of us in Jesus Christ. In fact, the idea that God knows us this well is a deep comfort indeed.

103. RELIABLE

"^{9}The Lord is a refuge for the oppressed,
  a stronghold in times of trouble.
^{10}Those who know your name trust in you,
  for you, Lord, have never forsaken those who seek you" (Psalm 9:9-10).

We all appreciate people who are reliable. They are the kind who do what they say they will do. Usually, they refuse requests because they also realize they might not be able to carry through on the task if they promise to fulfill it. We prefer to work with people who meet deadlines, get the job done according to our expectations. They are reliable.

Even reliable people, however, are stymied. Parents may promise a picnic to their children, but the weather can overrule them. Workers can promise to get a project done on schedule, but they can't control suppliers who ship late and delivery vehicles that break down along the way.

One reliable Person will always come through for us, though. He is the Lord God. He never lacks the strength to protect those whom He has promised to protect. He never wants for knowledge about what lies in the future so that His plans could be thwarted. Unlike the weather forecasters on TV, He is 100% accurate in His understanding of the future.

Best of all the features in the Lord God's reliability is the fact that He has never gone back on a promise He has made. Yes, He has made conditional promises which were ended when the conditions were violated by the fickle human beings with whom He had to deal; but God never showed a fickle side of Himself, not once! Whatever He promises us is more certain than the rising of the sun tomorrow morning.

David basked in the reliability of the Lord God. We bask in His reliability today.

The only uncertainty we have to address is this: Can God rely on me?

104. I WILL NOT LET GO!

"Then the man said, "Let me go, for it is daybreak."" But Jacob replied, "I will not let you go unless you bless me" (Genesis 32:26).

Jacob was a man covered with as many character flaws as a teenager with zits. He connived in an unfair bargain with his brother Esau. He deceived his father later for Esau's blessing. He did all he could to out cheat his Uncle Laban. He played favorites between his two wives and their sons. We could increase the list even more, but I think most people will get the idea.

Yet when it came to the preference the Lord expressed, He said He loved Jacob and hated Esau. Why? Well, when first we get an insight into Jacob's finagling we find him wanting Esau's birthright. The firstborn son received a double inheritance, and he received whatever blessings had been handed down to the father to hand down, in turn, to his son. These included the sure blessings of the Lord God upon Abraham and his descendants. Jacob was indeed a cheater. His name even meant "opportunist." But he cheated for the blessings of God.

He got bad marks for the means he used, but the Lord admired Jacob's desire for the blessings of God.

Skip ahead several years. Jacob is now returning to the land he fled when Esau had vowed to kill him. Esau is coming with 700 men as a welcoming committee. Jacob has earnestly prayed to the God Who told him to return to this land and asked that the Lord would deliver him from the hand of his brother, Esau. To put a safety buffer between himself and Esau's approaching force, Jacob sent Leah and her children first, Rachel and her son and servants second, and himself last. He has sent hundreds of livestock in recurring waves to overwhelm the brother from whom he had once stolen so much. Last, but not least, Jacob crossed the brook Jabbok to see if Esau would still be mad after all the gifts sent ahead of him.

Then a supernatural being fell upon Jacob, and they wrestled through the night. If ever you know what wrestling is like, you have to appreciate the stamina of this elderly patriarch. We know this "man" was supernatur-al because he simply touched Jacob's hip and threw it out of its socket. He wanted to get away before daybreak.

Still, Jacob held on, and the Angel of the Lord said, "Let me go, for day is breaking!"

To that Jacob replied, "I will not let you go unless you bless me."

The wrestling ceased, and the Lord blessed Jacob with a new name – Israel, the Prince of God.

I wonder at myself in this account. How long would I wrestle with spiritual forces to obtain a blessing? Would I still hold on when something as traumatic as a dislocated hip occurred in the struggle? Would I vow to hold on, no matter what, until I had obtained the Lord's blessing?

Time to go out on the wrestling mat and answer some soul-searching questions!

105. EXCHANGE RATE

"For He made him who knew no sin to be sin for us, that we might become the righteousness of God in Him" II Cor. 5:21.

A teenager was walking down the street with a toy poodle cuddled in his arms. He met his buddy along the way and said, "Hey! Look what I just got for my girl!"

His friend looked admiringly and said, "Man, how'd you ever arrange a trade like that?"

Speaking of incredible trades, Paul closes II Corinthians 5 with this verse that encapsulates the very Gospel message. God made the One Who knew no sin (Jesus) to become sin on behalf of us (sinners), so that we could be made the righteousness of God by Him.

This is a great deal for us! We did the crime. Jesus did the "hard time" for us. He was made the substitute sinner to die in the place of the deserving sinners.

But does it sound like a great deal for Jesus? Hebrews 12:2 tells us that for the glory of the joy set before Him He endured the cross. His greatest glory was to bring us into glory with Him! In the words of Max Lucado, "He would rather go to hell for you than go to heaven without you." It was a deal Jesus entered into knowingly, willingly, yes joyfully.

What makes you so special? It's the same thing that makes me so special: Jesus was willing to take my place. God prizes each one of us that much! The exchange rate may not make sense from our perspective, but it is the wellspring of true self-esteem. God thinks that highly of you that He would pay such an exchange rate.

106. BOTH HANDS

"For God so loved the world that He gave His only begotten Son, that whoever believes in Him should not perish but have everlasting life" (John 3:16 NKJV).

While I visited in Zimbabwe a few years ago, my host explained the protocol of giving and receiving a gift. Use both hands. When the giver gives the gift, he should present it with both hands; because that communicates to the recipient how much he values what he gives. It is precious, too precious to be treated casually or handled carelessly with one hand.

Likewise, the recipient should accept the gift with both hands. That says, "I value this gift you are giving me, and I will treasure it as some-thing very important in my life."

I like the custom I learned from the Shona people of Zimbabwe. It is a simple courtesy, similar to saying "Please" and Thank you." It costs so little to give and receive a gift in this manner, yet it communicates a powerful message: The giving and receiving of this gift is a significant event, not just a casual exchange between two parties which will soon be forgotten.

When God gave us His Greatest Gift He extended both hands.

Do we receive this gift in such a way that we communicate to Him how appreciative we are of the cost to Him and how much we will treasure it the rest of our lives?

107. HE MAKES ME TO LIE DOWN

"He makes me to lie down in green pastures" (Psalm 23:2a NKJV).

I write this particular devotion with my lower leg in a cast. I broke my leg over four months ago, and the term "patient" hardly seems appropriate for someone with my mindset. I try to calm my impatient heart with a reminder I myself have given to other patients when I have visited them in the hospital: Sometimes, the Good Shepherd makes us to lie down.

The Psalmist was himself a shepherd, and he understood something we "non-shepherds" don't appreciate. In order to ruminate, a necessary part of the digestive process for sheep, the sheep needs quiet time. The sheep cannot be agitated or on the move. It is best for him to lie down and be still. Then he brings up the cud and chews it.

We all need time out, occasionally, so we can ruminate. In Hebrew that's the same word that's used for meditating. When we read Psalm 23 and reflect on it, we certainly get the impression that David was doing some deep contemplating when he wrote it.

It's better for us to set aside time to ruminate, better for us to plan quiet times in the presence of the Good Shepherd than to wait until He makes us to lie down. We do this in regular devotions, in planned times of Bible study and prayer both alone and with others. We do it in our assembly around the Table of the Lord. We do it in habitually seeking God's face when we are engaged in mundane, non-stressful activity.

Never second guess the Lord. If He has made you to lie down recently, He has good reason to do so!

108. WHEN THE CALVARY CAME THROUGH

"Even so we, when we were children, were in bondage under the elements of the world. But when the fullness of the time had come, God sent forth His Son" (Galatians 4:3, 4a NKJV).

We tend to remember people for oddities of speech by which we could identify them. Elvis would acknowledge his audience's applause by saying, "Thank ya, thank ya vera much!" Or we identify Dirty Harry Callahan with some of the tag lines from his movies like, "Go ahead, make my day!" or "Do ya feel lucky? Well, do ya, punk?" Then there was the constant ribbing George W. Bush took for saying "nucuelar" instead of "nuclear."

My mother mispronounced a few words that still make me think of her. If we were watching a western where the Indians were about to overrun the heroes and a bugle sounded in the distance, she would say, "Here comes the calvary." I've heard a few other people confuse the terms too. Soldiers mounted on horses are called *cavalry*. *Calvary* is the name of the hill on which our Lord was crucified. Some may trust in horses, but we will trust in the Lord our God!

But Paul speaks of the timeliness of the redemptive work done on Calvary. All those living under rules alone are children subject to bondage, bondage to their desires, bondage to the guilt and penalty of sin. In our own strength, we were powerless, helpless, lost. At just the right time, God sent forth His Son to live out the sinless life under the Law no one else could live. This sinless One was injected into our sinful world. This perfect, powerful One took our imperfections and sins and nailed them to His cross, being condemned so we could go free.

My mom was right. At just the right time, the Calvary came to our rescue!

109. TRUTH AND LIES

"If we say that we have no sin, we deceive ourselves, and the truth is not in us. If we confess our sins, He is faithful and just to forgive us our sins and to cleanse us from all unrighteousness. If we say that we have not sinned, we make Him a liar, and His word is not in us" (I John 1:8-10).

Only sinners need to come to the Lord. Only the sick need a doctor. Those who cannot admit they have a need will never have their needs met.

Maybe it was a typo, but the following is an actual quote from the Brisbayne *Australian*: "Mr. John Hope, 42, a retired sea captain, was found on a beach near Flinders, Victoria with his hands tied together and his legs tied behind his back. Police investigating the death say that there appear to be no suspicious circumstances."

Really? Denial is more than just a River in Egypt!

To deny our sins, to say we don't need salvation, is to lie. To say Christ didn't need to die for us is to make Him out a liar! John makes it plain: To claim we have no sins from which to be saved keeps us in the "Lost" column. To come to Him willing to admit our sins qualifies us for the cleansing only His Blood can afford us.

110. THAT WHICH COST ME NOTHING

"Then the king said to Araunah, 'No, but I will surely buy it from you for a price; nor will I offer burnt offerings to the Lord my God with that which costs me nothing.'" (II Samuel 24:24a)

A hen and a hog watched from the barnyard as a billboard was put up across the road. "Enjoy the All American Breakfast," it said. "Eat ham and eggs at Ella's Diner!"

Commented the hen: "It's gratifying to realize we can each make a contribution to the American way of life, isn't it?"

"It may be a contribution for you," said the hog, "but it's a sacrifice for me!"

To turn back an awful plague threatening the land because David had committed a sin against the Lord, the prophet Gad told David to offer a sacrifice at the threshing floor of Araunah the Jebusite. When David went to the site and explained what he needed the site for, Araunah freely offered the land, the oxen with which he had been threshing, and wood for the fire. Araunah loved the king. He loved the Lord. He wished David well in his sacrifice.

But David understood the difference between a contribution and a sacrifice. The insisted on paying for it all. The amount he paid for the threshing floor and the oxen was generous. It was to be *David's* sacrifice, not Araunah's. In order for it to be that, it had to cost David and cost him dearly enough that there was no doubt his offering on the altar came from his heart. Appropriately, after David's sacrifice had been accepted at this place, David realized that it was to be the site of the Temple built to the glory of the God of Israel.

What Jesus gave on the cross was the ultimate Sacrifice on our behalf. While salvation has been freely offered to us, it was far from cheap for the Lord! As surely as a suitor would not propose to his beloved by giving her a zircon substitute for a diamond, neither would the Lord cheapen how dearly He valued each one of us by giving no less than His very best.

SPECIAL DAYS SECTION

IN REMEMBRANCE – UNTIL! (New Year)

Whenever the New Year rolls around, we spend time both looking back on the past year and looking forward to the year to come. We assess the things we have accomplished (and the things that didn't turn out that well). Then, we set goals we hope to accomplish in the coming year.

The Lord's Supper is intended to be the same kind of milestone. We look upon the past – our sins, our Savior, how dearly it cost Him to give us another chance at living and to provide the promise of undeserved Eternal Life in His presence. At the same time, we look forward to the "new chance" of living as we ought. We may not be there yet, but we're on the journey there. We may not have reached all of our goals, but we have goals to reach for; and that's better than when we lived for ourselves and nothing else.

The Bread and the Cup are a time of reflection on our Savior's Body and Blood. It was in His Body that Jesus suffered the pain we deserved. It was in His Blood that Jesus willingly poured out His very life so we could live forever. Yet even as He instituted this memorial feast, He declared, "I shall not drink of the fruit of the vine again until I drink it with you in my Father's Kingdom." Those who recall this understand there is still a day to come when the feast table shall be spread before all who have named Jesus as Lord and the Master Himself will raise the cup in toast to Eternity and drink it again – this time with all the brothers and sisters He has brought with Him!

"For as often as you eat this bread and drink this cup, you declare the Lord's death until He comes again" I Cor. 11:26.

PSALM SUNDAY (Palm Sunday)

"The stone the builders rejected has become the cornerstone; the Lord has done this, and it is marvelous in our eyes" (Psalm 118:22, 23).

The center of the Bible is found in the Book of Psalms.
The longest chapter in the Bible is Psalm 119 (176 verses).
The shortest chapter in the Bible is Psalm 117 (2 verses).
Add up all the chapters in the Bible, and the central chapter of the entire Bible is the Psalm between the longest and the shortest chapters, Psalm 118.

It is also the Psalm the worshippers were apparently singing when Jesus made His Triumphal Entry. It speaks of waving the festal boughs (v. 27) and includes the cry of "Hosanna!" ("Lord, save us!" v. 25). It is a Psalm about Messiah.

It is the Psalm referred to both by Jesus and His Disciples when they speak of the rejection of Jesus the Messiah by the Jewish leaders – "The stone the builders rejected has become the cornerstone."

Jesus, the Messiah, is the central theme of Scripture. It all points toward Him. To read the Bible and miss out on seeing Him is like reading a love letter and never knowing the person who sent it to you loves you! It's like reading a murder mystery and never finding out who did it.

How could a multitude of people cry "Hosanna! Blessed is He who comes in the name of the Lord!" on the First Day of the week and then be prompted to yell, "Crucify Him!" that Friday? If you go to the very center of the Bible, you should be able to see Jesus Christ. Sad enough, though, is the realization that a lot of people miss Him altogether.

ALIVE, DEAD, ALIVE FOREVERMORE (Easter)

"Do not be afraid. I am the First and the Last. I am He who lives, and was dead, and behold, I am alive forevermore. Amen. And I have the keys of Hades and Death" (Revelation 1:17, 18 [NKJV]).

When the Lord appeared to John at the beginning of the Revelation given to him, He spoke of the sequence of living, dying, and living forevermore. Jesus is elsewhere spoken of in the New Testament as being the "firstfruits" of those who rise from the dead.

The thing that appeals to me most, though, is the fact that He holds the keys to Hades and Death. Keys denote authority. When you get promoted in the firm, they give you the executive washroom key. When you are trusted in the bank, they give you the second key to the lockboxes in the vault. I remember how impressed the students were of me when I was a substitute teacher in the middle school because I had a full set of keys to every room in the building. You see, I was also a custodian once school dismissed there!

When Jesus said He held the keys to Hades and Death, He claimed an authority no one else could claim. Death could claim humans, but Jesus held the keys to release them from death! This is the ultimate authority to confirm Jesus' claim: "All power and authority has been given to me in Heaven and on earth."

We assemble on the First Day of the week because that was the day Jesus rose from the dead. Everything changed when He conquered Death forever.

BREAKING BREAD AND OPENED EYES (Easter)

"When he was at the table with them, he took bread, gave thanks, broke it and began to give it to them. Then their eyes were opened and they recognized him, and he disappeared from their sight" (Luke 24:30, 31).

A few years ago, I attended the funeral of the father of a friend of mine. As is so often the case, my attendance was not as much on behalf of the departed (whom I didn't even know), but for the son who was bereaved. I knew nothing of the preacher that day, but I was first amused to see the name of a man who had been a youth sponsor in our church during my teenage years. What a coincidence! But the name was common enough it wasn't hard to think there were two of them.

Just a few minutes into his talking, though, and I realized this was the same person – considerably older than he looked when I was young, but the same person. My eyes were opened to recognize him as I heard him speak.

The resurrection appearance of Jesus to Cleopas and his companion along the Emmaus road is recorded only in Luke. It is also the only resurrection appearance we find of Jesus appearing to someone who is named only the one time in the resurrection appearance. We never heard of Cleopas before. We never hear of him again.

We also read another interesting contrast: Jesus went unrecognized all the way along the road. As they later recounted His appearance they remarked about how listening to Him expound on all that the prophets had said about Messiah suffering before He would enter into His glory caused their hearts to burn within them. They had listened to an A-1 class Bible exposition from the Risen Christ, probably for a couple of hours or so.

And they still didn't recognize Him!

When were their eyes finally opened? It happened around the table, as He gave thanks for the bread and broke it.

The early church met "for the breaking of bread" according to Acts 20:7. The focus of the assembly at first for the church was not for the sermon, but for communion! It is in the breaking of bread that disciples' eyes are opened and they catch a glimpse of Jesus.

THE AUNT AND THE GRANDMA (Mother's Day)

"When Athaliah the mother of Ahaziah saw that her son was dead, she proceeded to destroy the whole royal family. But Jehosheba, the daughter of King Jehoram and sister of Ahaziah, took Joash son of Ahaziah and stole him away from among the royal princes, who were about to be murdered. She put him and his nurse in a bedroom to hide him from Athaliah; so he was not killed" (II Kings 11:1-2).

She taught her own sons and their friends to be bank robbers. Such was the legacy of Kate "Ma" Barker during the Depression. Likewise, she died in a hail of bullets in Florida along with the other men she had "mothered" once the FBI caught up with her.

I bet you never expected to hear someone like her mentioned on Mother's Day, did you?

Giving birth fulfills the biological aspects of being a mother, but the mothers we honor on this day understand that giving birth is but the beginning of the task of mothering. Indeed, there are many adopted children this day who honor mothers who never gave birth to them.

During the period of the Divided Kingdom, we find a plot within Judah so dark and sinister we could only conclude that Satan himself was behind it! The royal line of David was all but completely eliminated by the daughter of Jezebel. Athaliah was not just the daughter of Jezebel and mother of Ahaziah; she was also the grandmother of all the princes she ruthlessly had killed so she could usurp the throne!

She almost succeeded, except for one godly person, Jehosheba the wife of Jehoiada the High Priest. Jehosheba was sister to Ahaziah, making her the aunt of the baby she rescued from the queen's murderous plot. She hid the boy in her bedchamber and later raised him as her own son in her own household until he could ascend to the throne. King Joash was the single thread that kept alive the line of David – hence the Promised Messiah as well.

"Grandma" Athaliah was ambitious and murderous. Grandparents don't normally behave the way she did. She was the "Ma Barker" of Old Testament history. In stark contrast is the faithful aunt who raised a boy in her house as if he were her own son. She prepared Joash to reign on the throne of David, which he did well all the years her husband was able to advise him!

Not a biological mother? Never underestimate the call of mothering a child not born to you! It takes more than giving birth to make a woman a good mother.

BE GENTLE WITH THE YOUNG MAN (Father's Day)

"The king commanded Joab, Abishai and Ittai, 'Be gentle with the young man Absalom for my sake.'" – II Samuel 18:5a

When we engage in spiritual warfare on behalf of our King, we need to discern His greatest wishes. The King's heart yearns for the wayward, rebellious child.

David's commanders heard his statement even as they marshaled their forces against the son who had taken over Jerusalem and pursued his father. The troops heard the command given, as well. Yet, when Absalom was trapped by the branches of an oak which had caught his head he was killed by David's commander of all the troops.

Discerning the Lord's Body includes understanding just who it was that Jesus died for – the heroin addict, the porn stars, the obnoxious atheists. We are not marching into battle against them. We are on a rescue mission to free them from their captor. Winning an argument with an atheist is easier than winning the atheist. Shaming a sinner is easier than rescuing a sinner.

The Father's heart yearns for the wayward child. Deal gently with him, for the Father's sake!

ABUNDANCE AMNESIA (Thanksgiving)

"When you have eaten and are satisfied, praise the Lord your God for the good land he has given you. Be careful that you do not forget the Lord your God, failing to observe his command, his laws and his decrees that I am giving you this day" (Deuteronomy 8:10-11).

Severe trauma has been known most frequently to cause amnesia. Sometimes the events of a terrible accident or crime will cause the victim to "blank out" all the details of the most horrific moments of the terrible event. Sometimes, it is referred to as "hysteric amnesia."

But who would've thought that having an abundance would make us forgetful? Moses said it was likely to happen when Israel finally took possession of the land of plenty and lived in houses they never built and ate from fig trees and grape vines they had never planted.

When we are blessed materially, we tend to be drawn away by attention to the "things" we possess. In truth, "things" possess us even more than we will ever possess them. We have to lock them up, protect them from the weather, keep them in proper maintenance, even put them to use because of how valuable they are! The "things" we claim to own have a way of dictating to us that we will give them attention.

While we give attention to the things, our focus can be drawn away from those who have given them to us or made it possible for us to acquire them. When we forget those who have made our possession of material blessings possible, we are guilty of ingratitude.

We celebrate Thanksgiving not to watch football or practice annual gluttony with relatives. The real purpose of Thanksgiving is to remember the One Who gave us our blessings. It is a grievous sin to focus on the things and forget the Giver of every good gift.

We celebrate the Lord's Supper for the same reason. It is not simply material stuff that we have received from God's hand. We have eternal life, the forgiveness of sins, the indwelling Holy Spirit to empower us to live holy and godly lives in Christ Jesus. We dare not forget the Giver as we bask in the joy of His great gifts to us!

FEAR NOT! (Christmas)

"But the angel said to them, 'Do not be afraid. I bring you good news of great joy that will be for all the people'" (Luke 2:9).

It seems almost every time an angel appears with a message for people, he has to preface the message with "Fear not!" That was the case here, where the angel of the Lord appeared to the shepherds taking care of their flocks on the hillside just outside of Bethlehem.

When angels appear in the Bible, they are not effeminate. They are not the kind of being which inspires a warm, gushy feeling. The glory of the Lord shone all around these shepherds when the angle appeared, and they were terrified. The same thing happened the morning of Jesus' resurrection at the Garden Tomb. Roman soldiers were so afraid of the mere appearance of the angel from heaven they shook and were paralyzed in their fear!

If an angel appeared here this morning in similar fashion, you can bet we would also be petrified in fear of what such a being could do, if he wanted to deal with sin-tainted humans as they deserve.

But visiting heavenly wrath upon these shepherds wasn't the angel's mission. He said his mission was to give them a Gospel. That's what "good news" means.

It wasn't the Gospel of redemption accomplished on the Cross, because it wasn't accomplished yet. But it was the good news of the birth of Messiah. He ultimately would redeem us from sin, and His coming was worthy of celebration. Still, there was reason not to fear. Messiah came as a baby, not as a King on a charger to execute wrath on His enemies. We have good cause not to be afraid

MESSY WOMEN (Christmas)

"A record of the genealogy of Jesus Christ the son of David, the son of Abraham:…" (Matthew 1:1)

Did you ever do genealogical research? In so doing, did you ever find some things in your family history you wish you hadn't found? Somewhere in my family, there is a book giving facts about my ancestors: birth date, death date, spouse, children, life's accomplishments. One name has a simple statement following it – "He was a horse thief!"

Four women are mentioned in the genealogy of Jesus Christ:

1. Tamar (Matt. 1:3) pretended to be a cult prostitute to fool her widowed father-in-law to impregnate her.
2. Rahab (Matt. 1:5) was the prostitute in Jericho who hid the spies and in so doing bartered for her family's lives when the city fell.
3. Ruth (Matt. 1:5) was a Moabitess, a descendant of Lot, by an incestuous relationship with his own daughter.
4. Uriah's wife (Matt. 1:6) was Bathsheba. We know the story of David and Bathsheba, don't we?

Granted, each story is more complicated than the shady backgrounds around these women; and many are remembered for faith and courage that reached beyond scandal. All the same, the scandals are there as a part of the genealogy.

The woman who gave birth to Jesus did so in the shadow of great scandal too. Mary took social scorn for getting pregnant before she was married. She had no guarantees from Gabriel about what would become of her engagement to Joseph when she agreed to bear Messiah, and Joseph would have called it all off if it hadn't been for God's special intervention.

For all the decorations and lovely trimmings, Christmas is also messy. Boxes, wrappings, food scraps, dirty dishes clutter the house. The birth of Jesus is told to us with all the messes laid bare. He was born of a family line with its own catalog of scandals. If His genealogy had been impeccable, we would always have wondered whether or not we could identify with Him, so He made sure that He first identified with us, with our genealogies with horse thieves and other scandals.

And that is the genius of the Incarnation. Since we were powerless to regain the Image of God we had tarnished with sin, God became one of us. The only way He could get us out of our mess was for Him to come down into it and lift us up.

WHAT DO THESE STONES MEAN? (Memorial Day)

"This may be a sign among you when your children ask in time to come, saying, 'What do these stones mean to you?' Then you shall answer them that the waters of the Jordan were cut off before the ark of the covenant of the Lord; when it crossed over the Jordan, the waters of the Jordan were cut off. And these stones shall be a memorial to the children of Israel forever." (Josh. 4:6, 7).

Memorial Day is marked in Arlington Cemetery by the President's placing of a wreath at the Tomb of the Unknowns. We have markers in that cemetery for many famous soldiers and statesmen, and all of those graves are likewise decorated on this weekend. It is appropriate to remember these great people as a means of recognizing the price soldiers have paid in battle to secure the blessings of liberty for us. We need to remind ourselves. We need to remind the generations that follow us.

Joshua set up a memorial to the crossing of the Jordan River into the Promised Land. This journey had started 40 years earlier with the parting of the Red Sea. It culminated here, with the parting of the Jordan River and crossing into the Promised Land. Wisely, Joshua had strong men, one from each tribe, to gather a large stone from the dried river bed before the Jordan flowed again. The stones were stacked into a monument to commemorate this great event. In the future, people would remember what happened at this stretch of the Jordan River.

The night before He died, Jesus wisely established a memorial to the pivotal point of all human history. Now, when our children ask us what this time is all about, we explain the loaf and the cup. We describe all that Jesus suffered in His body because of our sins, how His very life was poured out in His blood, the way the fruit of the vine is poured out into the cup. It is a point of remembrance for us, a teachable moment for our sons and daughters.

Made in the USA
Las Vegas, NV
05 April 2024

88270147R00072